16576

Jan 28, 2003

423.

423. 031   16576

DATE DUE

APR 2 2 2013	

BRODART, INC.   Cat. No. 23-221

D1443139

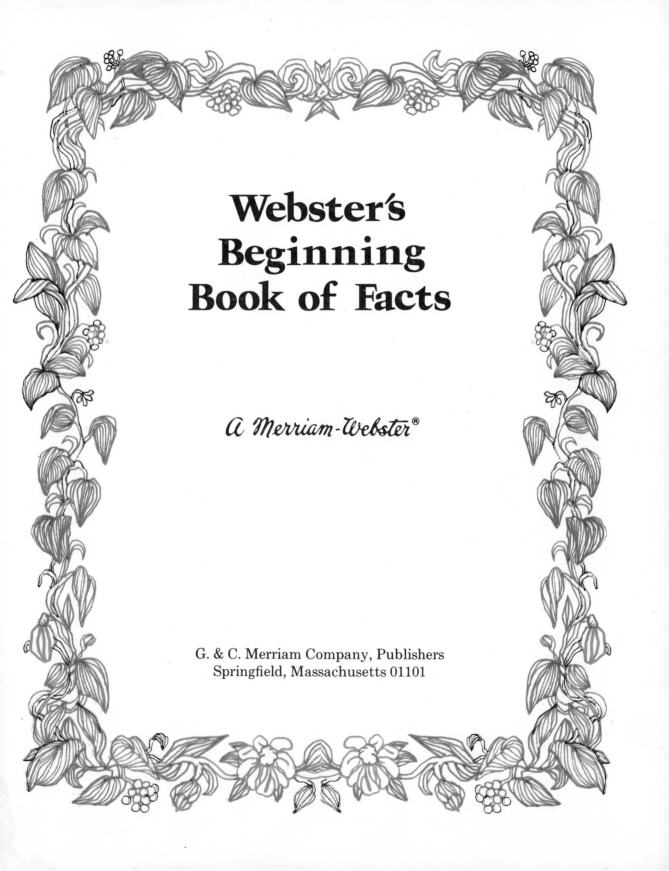

Webster's
Beginning
Book of Facts

A Merriam-Webster®

G. & C. Merriam Company, Publishers
Springfield, Massachusetts 01101

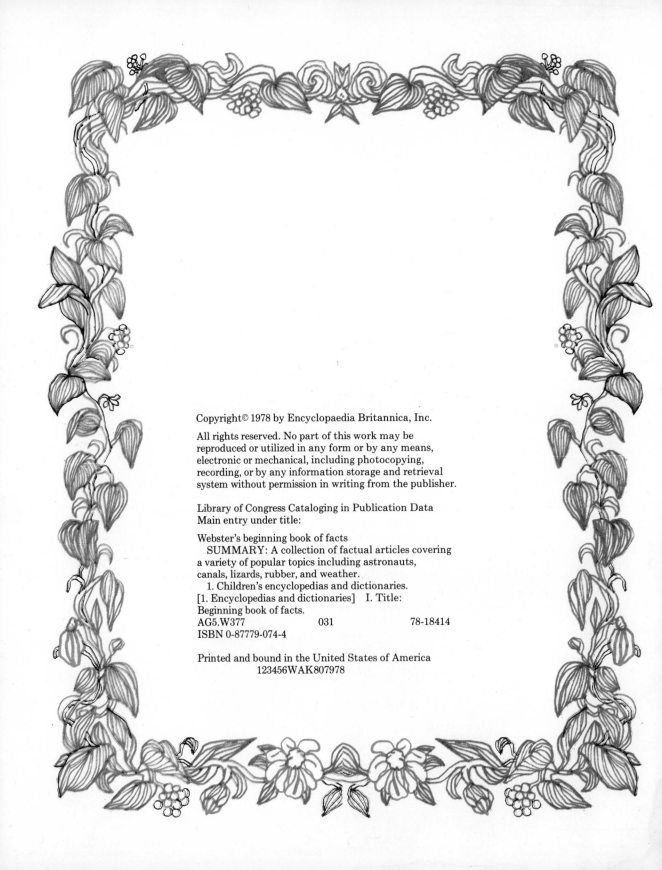

Copyright© 1978 by Encyclopaedia Britannica, Inc.

All rights reserved. No part of this work may be
reproduced or utilized in any form or by any means,
electronic or mechanical, including photocopying,
recording, or by any information storage and retrieval
system without permission in writing from the publisher.

Library of Congress Cataloging in Publication Data
Main entry under title:

Webster's beginning book of facts
  SUMMARY: A collection of factual articles covering
a variety of popular topics including astronauts,
canals, lizards, rubber, and weather.
   1. Children's encyclopedias and dictionaries.
[1. Encyclopedias and dictionaries]   I. Title:
Beginning book of facts.
AG5.W377   031   78-18414
ISBN 0-87779-074-4

Printed and bound in the United States of America
      123456WAK807978

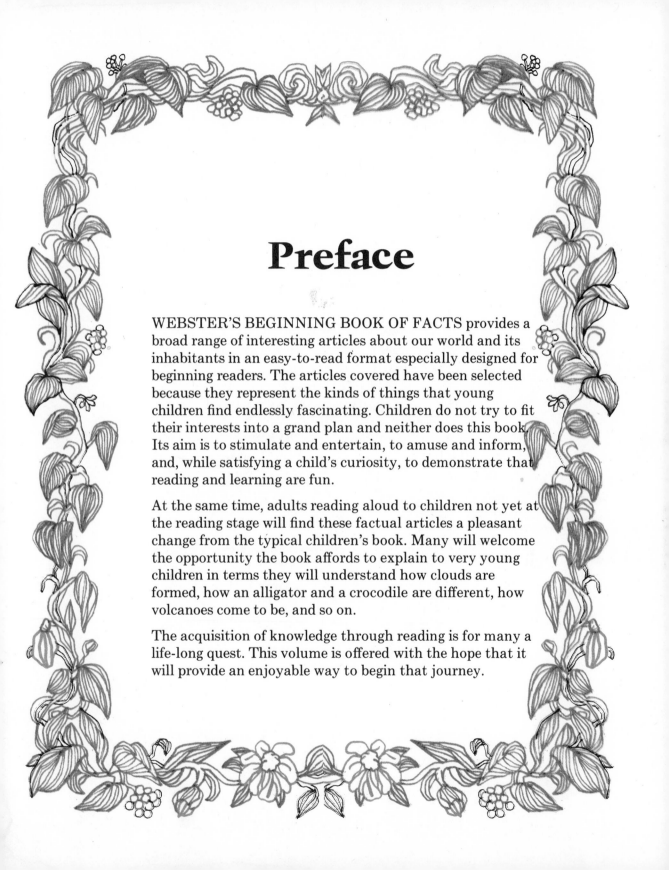

Preface

WEBSTER'S BEGINNING BOOK OF FACTS provides a broad range of interesting articles about our world and its inhabitants in an easy-to-read format especially designed for beginning readers. The articles covered have been selected because they represent the kinds of things that young children find endlessly fascinating. Children do not try to fit their interests into a grand plan and neither does this book. Its aim is to stimulate and entertain, to amuse and inform, and, while satisfying a child's curiosity, to demonstrate that reading and learning are fun.

At the same time, adults reading aloud to children not yet at the reading stage will find these factual articles a pleasant change from the typical children's book. Many will welcome the opportunity the book affords to explain to very young children in terms they will understand how clouds are formed, how an alligator and a crocodile are different, how volcanoes come to be, and so on.

The acquisition of knowledge through reading is for many a life-long quest. This volume is offered with the hope that it will provide an enjoyable way to begin that journey.

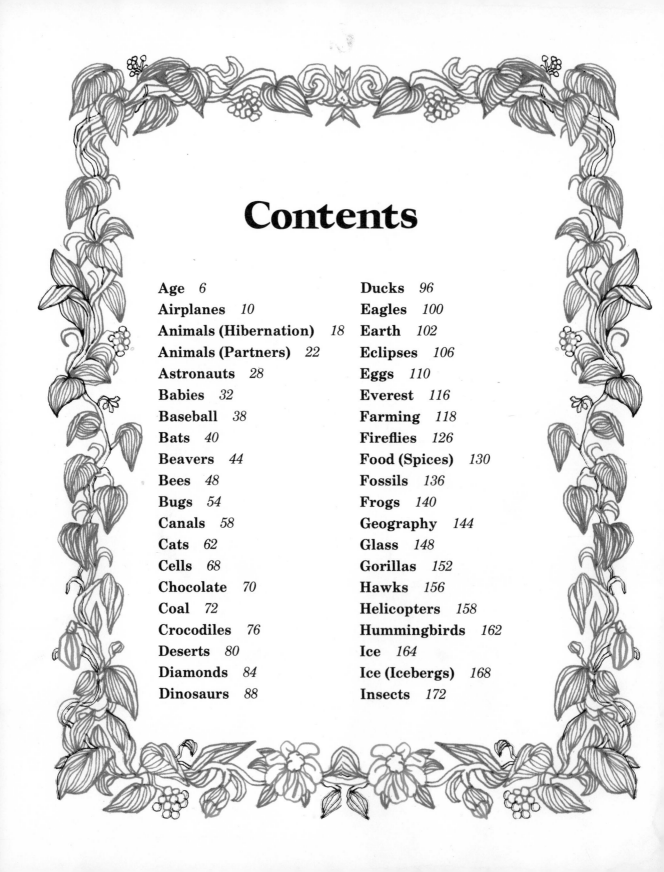

Contents

How Many Birthdays?

Johnny has grown!

He's a whole inch taller than he was on his last birthday. And he's grown bigger *around,* as well as *up.*

If we know how tall Johnny is and how much he weighs, we might be able to guess how old he is. But we can't be absolutely sure unless we ask, because growing boys and girls of any age come in many different sizes and shapes.

Trees have birthdays, too. And even though a tree can't talk, we can still find out how old it is. How? By looking at the end of a tree that has been cut down.

As new wood grows inside the bark of the tree, the tree becomes taller and bigger around. Each year one new band, or *ring*, of wood grows, making the tree trunk wider. The color of the new wood is usually a little different from the color of the last year's ring of wood. If we count these rings on the end of a tree, we learn how many years the tree lived.

A sheep doesn't look much like a tree, does it? But in one way they're alike. If you could ever catch a certain kind of wild mountain sheep and look at its curling horns, do you know what you'd see? Bumpy rings—one ring for each birthday the sheep has had.

You can even tell how many birthdays some fish have had.

As this fish grows older and thicker and longer, the scales that cover its skin become larger. Each year a ringlike mark forms on each scale. We can tell how old some fish are by counting the rings on their scales.

Most fish and sheep don't live as long as people. And people don't live as long as some trees.

How many years can a person live? We're not sure. But we do know that some people live to be more than 100 years old. What if you had to light 100 candles on a cake—could you blow them all out with one breath?

The things that live the longest are trees. Some trees live to be thousands of years old. To find room for the candles on the birthday cake of one of those trees, we would need a cake as big as a house!

Before There Were Planes

For a long time people wanted to fly, but no one knew how. Some people may have tried flapping their arms, as if they were birds.

They flapped and jumped, and flopped and bumped.

"Feathers!" someone thought. "What we need is feathers!"

And so some adventurous people made large, feathery, fluffy wings and strapped the wings to their arms. *Flap! . . . flap!* But no one left the ground.

"Aha!" someone else thought, "we'll start from high above the ground, the way a bird flies from its nest. Then we'll fly!"

They flapped and jumped, and flopped and bumped.

Some broke their bones when they fell. Others were killed. They all learned that feathers can't help people fly.

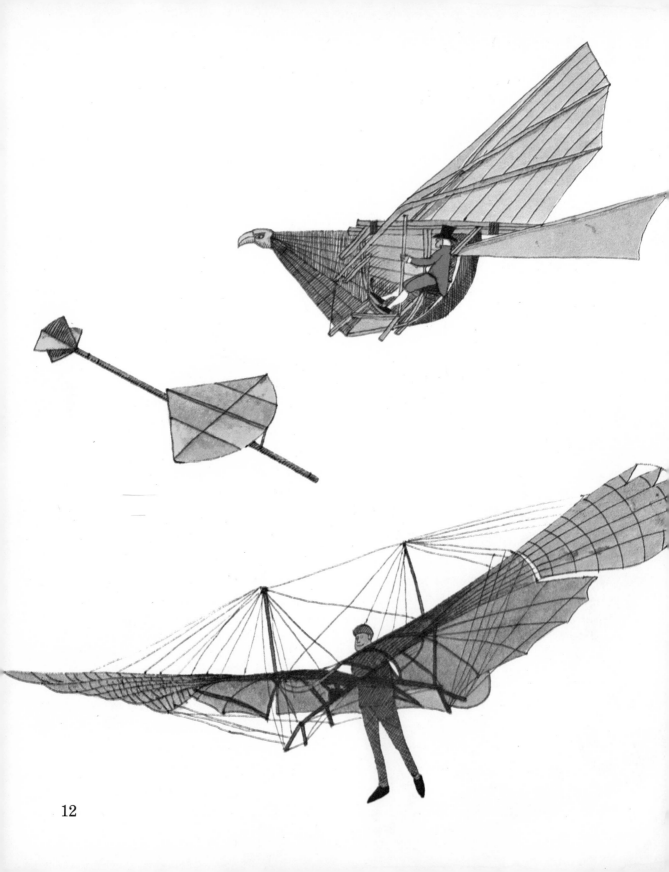

Then one day while watching a kite, someone had an exciting idea. "We'll build a kite big enough to carry a man up in the air!"

It worked!

"I know!" someone else probably said. "We'll take the string off the kite . . . and make the kite bigger . . . and add wings like a bird's. Then maybe it will glide through the air like a soaring bird."

It did! And now people had a kite-plane, or *glider*.

After people put engines on wagons to make the first automobiles, inventors wondered if an engine on a glider would help it stay up in the air. On their first tries, they built some very strange machines. One looked like a bat. It shook and roared and bounced and rattled and did nearly everything except fly!

Two brothers named Orville and Wilbur Wright built a flying machine in their bicycle shop. It had the strong, light wings of a glider. And it also had a gasoline engine and two propellers.

The brothers took their machine to a large, sandy beach near the ocean. Orville lay flat on the lower wing, ready to guide the machine. Wilbur started it.

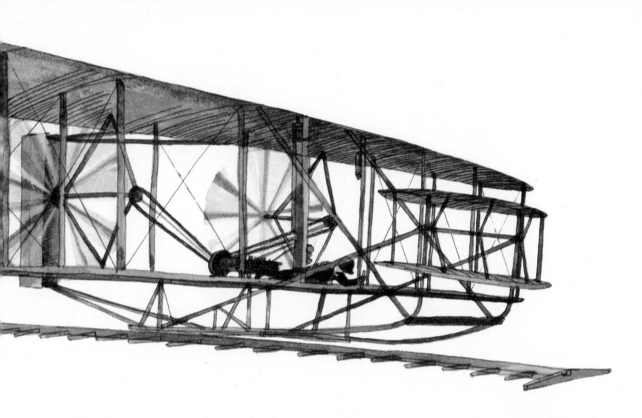

The engine roared. The propellers spun. The plane shook as though it might fall apart. It rolled down the beach and then, suddenly, rose into the air. It bobbed up and down and from side to side like a kite without enough tail, but it flew for 12 seconds before it came down in the sand.

At last, man had learned to fly!

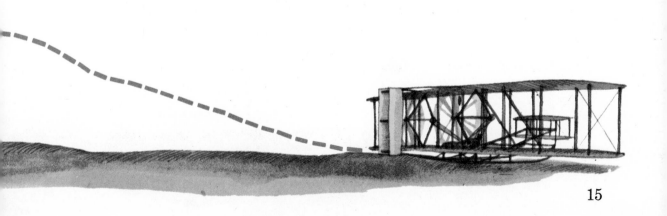

The astonishing news was too much for some people to believe. But it was true, and soon other inventors were proving it again and again. Each time a new kind of plane was built, we learned a little more about flying.

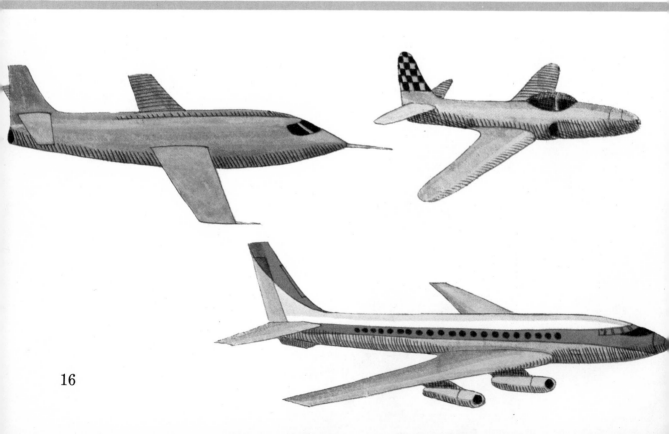

We learned that airplanes fly faster when they are built with the smooth, simple shape of a bird in flight.

Today some airplanes look very much like birds. But they fly faster and farther and higher than any bird.

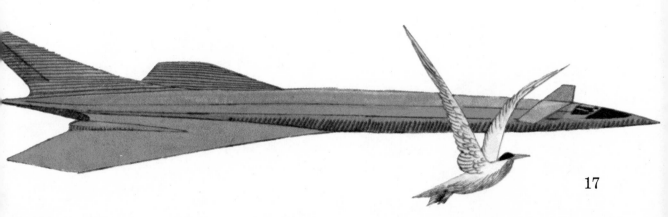

The Special Long Sleep

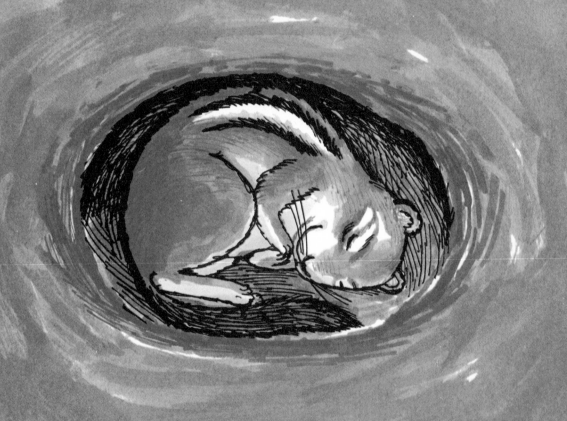

What's this ground squirrel doing?

It looks as if it's just asleep for the night, but it's not. It's not pretending, either. It's *hibernating*.

Hibernating is a special lo-o-o-ng sleep. This ground squirrel has gone to sleep for the whole winter.

How can it do this? Doesn't it need to eat?

No.

Why doesn't it?

When they're running around, animals *do* need food—just as cars need gasoline. Without gasoline, a car stops. Without food, an animal can live for only a short time. Then it will die.

In the summer there's usually plenty of food for animals to eat.

In the winter there's less food to be found. Some animals go south, where it's warmer, and find food there. Some bury nuts and seeds under the ground in the summertime, and in the winter they can dig them up.

Other animals do as the ground squirrel does. They go to sleep for most of the winter—they hibernate.

Woodchucks, hamsters, bats, and hedgehogs are some of the other animals that can hibernate. Some birds, fish, insects, and butterflies hibernate, too.

When an animal takes its special long sleep, its heart almost stops beating. Its blood almost stops flowing. It gets very, very cold, almost—but not quite—cold enough to freeze. And it almost stops breathing. Some hibernating animals take only one breath every few minutes.

When the weather gets warm again, the heart of the hibernating animal begins to beat faster. The blood runs faster. The animal breathes faster, too. Its body becomes warm. It gets up and goes to join the other animals looking for food. It is spring!

In fairy tales and legends, such as "Sleeping Beauty" and "Rip Van Winkle," we read about people who sleep for a very long time. Rip Van Winkle slept for 20 years, and when he woke up, he found that everything had changed. He had become an old man with a white beard.

In real life, people can't hibernate. They get hungry and wake up ready for breakfast.

But some scientists think that maybe sometime we *can* find a way to hibernate. Then we could get in a spaceship and "go to sleep" and wake up a long time later on a star.

SCHLEICHER CO. PUBLIC LIBRARY
BOX 611 — PH. 853-3767
ELDORADO, TEXAS 76936

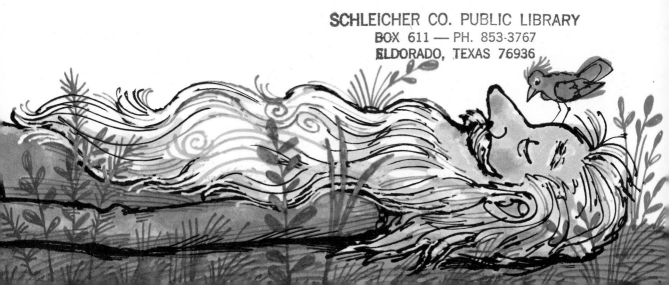

Animal Partners

Snap!

No, that's not the huge jaws of the crocodile clamping down on the little plover bird. It's the beak of the plover snatching food from between the wrinkles of the crocodile's thick skin.

In a way, the giant crocodile and the tiny bird are friends. They help each other. The bird picks off leeches and other bothersome water creatures that stick to the crocodile's skin. Sometimes the crocodile dozes with its frightful mouth open. Some people say the bird even goes inside its mouth to look for leeches or to pick food from between its teeth.

The bird pays the crocodile for its meals by squawking loudly when enemies are near, and the crocodile is warned.

A lizard and a bird called the *petrel* are friends, too. They even live together in a nest under the ground. The petrel builds the nest. The lizard keeps it clean by eating lice and other pests that keep creeping in.

Although the nest is not large, each has enough room to sleep. That's because the lizard stays at home and keeps house all day while the bird is out flying around. Then, when the bird wings its way home at night, the lizard goes out hunting.

A zebra and an ostrich—now there's a nice pair. Zebras and ostriches sometimes roam together and take turns warning each other when danger is near.

On sunny days the ostrich, which can see much better and farther than the zebra, is the lookout, or scout.

On cloudy days or when it's growing dark, the zebra is the leader. The zebra hears better and has a sharper sense of smell than the ostrich. When it gets too dark to see, the zebra uses its ears and nose.

The big horn of an angry rhinoceros is one of the most dangerous weapons in the world. With its horn a rhinoceros can butt
down a tree. It can protect itself from lions and tigers. Most
people and creatures stay away from a rhinoceros—except for one
little bird.

This bird is the rhino's partner. It is always welcome to perch
on the rhino's back. That's because the bird sits there and eats
the tiny insects that bite and bore into the hide of the great beast.
The insects are called *ticks*. The bird is known as the *tickbird*.

So—because it hates the ticks that a tickbird likes—even the
dangerous rhino has a friend.

The little bird called a *honey guide* flies high over the trees and bushes looking for a hive or a hollow tree where the bees keep their honey.

When the honey guide sees the hive, it flies quickly to a small furry animal called a *ratel*.

By chattering loudly from the air, the honey guide leads the ratel to the honeycomb.

Now it's time for the ratel to do its share of the work. It tears into the bees' nest with its strong, sharp claws. Its heavy, black-and-white fur protects it from the angry bees.

After the ratel has eaten its fill and scared some of the bees away, it's the honey guide's turn.

These are just a few of the creatures that help each other. Some are strong; some are weak. Some are fast; some are slow. Some are big; some are small.

A Walk in Space

The first man to walk in outer space was a Russian, Aleksei Leonov. Leonov didn't actually *walk* in space with his feet. In space there is no earth under your feet to walk on. There is nothing under your feet at all.

Leonov *floated* in space. When he wanted to move, he would tug on a line that was wrapped around him and fastened to the spaceship. One tug and he would float where he wanted to go.

Leonov took pictures during his space walk. When he finished, he pushed his camera toward the spaceship. It floated through the spaceship door. So did Leonov.

The first American to step into outer space was Edward White. White used a jet gun to help him move where he wanted to go. His jet gun pushed him much as a jet engine pushes an airplane. It's something like the way a toy balloon moves when air rushes out.

White had a line around him, too. His line, like Leonov's, carried fresh air for him to breathe, and messages from inside his spaceship and from Earth.

The line also kept him from moving too far away from his ship. It would be easy to move too fast and drift so far into space that it would be hard to get back. At one time White took off his outer gloves during his space walk so he could work more easily. One glove floated away before he could catch it.

It is very quiet in space. And very large and empty. Close your eyes, stay very quiet, and imagine that the darkness you see goes on and on. You will have some idea of what space is like.

In space there is no up or down. You can float on your stomach . . . or on your back . . . or on your head—and it all feels the same. It doesn't make any difference to you whether you look at the Earth upside down or right side up.

The easiest thing to do in space is tumble and spin over and over in giant somersaults. Throw a ball in space and you'll fly backward while the ball goes forward. Put a big wrench on a bolt that is part of a platform in space. Start to turn the bolt. If you aren't careful you may find your whole body spinning around with the turning bolt. If you just pushed against the outside of a spaceship with your little finger, you would scoot backwards in space *and keep going*. Unless you had something like a rocket gun with you to control your direction, or unless someone came and got you, you'd never, never stop.

Leonov and White were the first men to work outside of a space capsule. Their experiments were a first step toward the building of space stations that are necessary for the exploration of outer space. A small space station can be launched from Earth. But larger space stations, such as the one shown here, will have to be built in outer space from materials rocketed from Earth.

Biggest Family

A mother fish lays more eggs than you can count—often more than a million. She doesn't stay to take care of the baby fish that come from the eggs. After she drops her eggs in the water, she swims away.

When a baby fish comes out of one of the eggs, it has *hatched*. But not many of the eggs do hatch. Other fish—and frogs and turtles—eat many of the fish eggs. Some of the eggs float onto the land, where birds eat them.

A mother bird usually lays
only as many eggs as can be kept
warm with her body — usually
four or five eggs. After they're
hatched, she feeds and protects
the baby birds and helps them
learn to fly.

Very large animals, such as horses and cows and elephants,
almost always have only one baby at a time.

But small animals, such as mice and rabbits and opossums, have
several babies at a time.

A mother hamster can have as many as 12 babies—a dozen—about every month. And in just a few weeks, those babies can start having babies of their own—often every month!

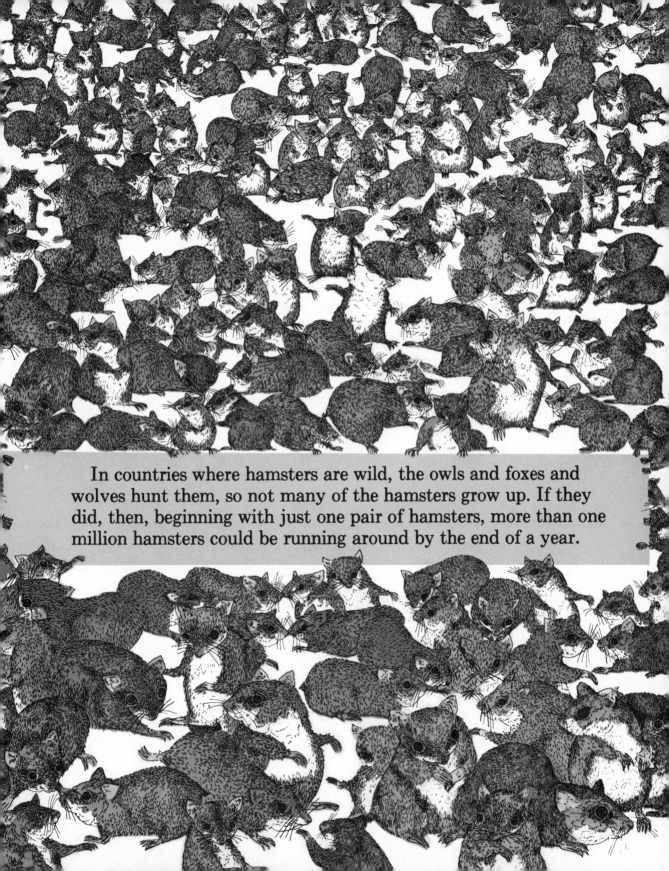

In countries where hamsters are wild, the owls and foxes and wolves hunt them, so not many of the hamsters grow up. If they did, then, beginning with just one pair of hamsters, more than one million hamsters could be running around by the end of a year.

Boys and girls are almost always born one at a time.

When they're born two at a time, they're called *twins*.

When they're born three at a time, they're called *triplets*.

When they're born four at a time, they're called *quadruplets*.

Once in a great, great while they're born five at a time, and then they're called *quintuplets*.

Babies grow slowly, and they grow for a long time. And during all this time their parents take care of them and keep them safe and try to help them grow up happily.

It takes a long time before a human family can grow this big.

How Pitchers Fool Batters

"Strike two!" the umpire shouts.

The batter waits, wiggling his bat, ready to swing. The pitcher lifts his arms, stretches, and throws the ball. The batter swings and misses! It's a strikeout!

Even good batters sometimes strike out in baseball. The reason is that the pitcher never lets the batter know what kind of pitch he is going to throw. Sometimes he throws as hard as he can, sometimes not so hard, sometimes not hard at all. And sometimes he tricks the batter by making the ball curve a little bit as it nears home plate.

Most of the time—whether he throws a fast ball or a slow ball—the pitcher holds the ball the same way, with his first two fingers and thumb. But when he throws a curve or a slider (pitches that curve the ball toward or away from the batter), he holds the ball a little differently. He throws the curve with a twist of the wrist, letting the ball slide out from between his thumb and his first finger. That makes the ball spin, and the spin makes it curve.

A pitcher may hold the ball in still a different way—for a very special pitch. He takes the ball in his fingertips, using all his fingers, and just barely holds it with his fingernails. The pitcher looks as if he is throwing it hard; yet the ball comes very slowly and does not spin at all. You might think a pitch that does not spin at all would come straight across the plate, but it doesn't. Instead, air currents catch the seams of the ball—the places where it is sewn together—and make it turn right or left and bob up or down. Even the pitcher doesn't know exactly which way it is going to turn, and the batter can only guess.

BATS

It Flies, but It's Not a Bird

If bats could think about what kind of animal they are, they probably would be surprised to find out that they are not birds.

Bats are the only furry animals that can fly—without using an airplane, that is.

A bat's wings are really just long, thin fingers with a piece of skin—called a *membrane*—stretched between them.

A bat's wings have no feathers. A bat's body looks something like a mouse's body and is covered with soft fur.

A bat doesn't even have a bird's bill. It has a mouth with tiny, sharp teeth in it. It has a nose and furry ears. Some people call a bat a flying mouse—although it really isn't.

Bats fly very well with their unusual wings. You probably have seen them flying around in the early evening, zigging and zagging as they catch mosquitoes in the air. The insect-eating bats are very helpful to people. They eat billions and billions of harmful insects.

Other bats eat fruit or pollen from flowers. Some even catch small fish and eat them.

There are bats of many different colors. Most are brown, but some are blackish, orange, gray, grayish green, greenish white, red, or yellowish. Some are spotted or have two colors.

The large vampire bats, which live in hot jungles, can suck blood from other animals. They often carry germs that can make people sick, so people keep away from them. But most bats don't hurt anything except mosquitoes and other insects.

Bats can't see very well in the bright sunlight, so they sleep all day, hanging upside down in dark places, such as caves, hollow trees, and barns. They fly at night.

They can fly in places where it is so dark that they can't see. And yet, even in the pitch dark, they almost never bump into anything.

Why don't they?

Because they send out sounds as they fly. They aren't sounds that people can hear. But bats can hear them. The sounds go ahead of the flying bats and bounce back from anything that might be in their way. By hearing the echoes, bats can tell where things are in the dark.

In the north some bats *hibernate*—sleep a special long sleep—all winter long. Other northern bats, such as the red bat, simply fly to warmer places during the winter.

A baby bat drinks milk from its mother's breasts, as puppies or kittens do. When it is very young, the mother carries it with her. It clings to her fur as she flies through the air, searching for food.

44

The Busy Animal

This furry creature zigs and zags, twists and turns, as it skims through the water, using its back feet as flippers.

Picking up just the right size sticks and rocks for building its house, this animal has front feet that work as hands do.

It has a long, flat tail shaped like a canoe paddle—just right for steering in water and for leaning on when this fellow is gnawing down a tree.

Have you guessed what this animal is? It's a beaver—small, strong, and probably the cleverest builder in the animal world.

Without a saw, an ax, or a knife, a beaver can cut down a tree so big you couldn't wrap your arms around the trunk! It uses trees to build a dam across a river, making a private pond for beaver families.

How do beavers do all this hard work? Well, if you could look inside a beaver's mouth—don't try it, you'd get bitten!—you would see very long, very sharp front teeth. So long and so sharp that they can gnaw around a tree trunk in no time at all.

Crunch! Crack! Smash! Crash! Another tree ready for the beaver to gnaw into sticks and logs. (A beaver's front teeth aren't just sharp and strong—they never wear out. They keep right on growing as long as a beaver lives!)

Sometimes beavers manage to gnaw down a tree so that it falls
in the water. But if it misses, the beavers don't seem to be
bothered. They dig a canal—a water path—cut the tree into logs
with their teeth, and float the logs to the right place for building
a dam.

Beavers work much as construction workers do. Each has a job.
When all the logs are pushed together, the beavers plaster the
cracks with mud and rocks.

Time for a rest? Not for beavers. It's time for house building!
Scurrying back and forth to gather sticks and stones . . . clawing
for mud to pack their houses tight and safe . . . beavers make
wonderful houses.

A snug dry room above the water is lined with moss and soft
shredded bark—perfect for raising beaver babies.

The storage place for winter food is underwater. Beavers don't waste any part of a tree—they even use the bark for food!

If you should see one beaver, you can be sure that other beavers are close by. They build together. They live together. And they stay safe together!

If a beaver spots an enemy (wildcats and wolves hunt beavers for food, but men hunt them for their silky fur), it slaps its tail as hard as it can on the water. *Smack!* Beavers know that sound means trouble. They race for the water, dive in, and swim out to their houses.

Are you ever "busy as a beaver"?

"Busy as a beaver" is an old, old saying that means working hard. And no one seems to work harder than beavers!

Honeybee at Work

B-z-z-z-z-z-z-z-z-z-z-z-z-z-z. . . .
Honeybee at work!
The bee flies from blossom to blossom, gathering food for other bees. And without knowing it, the bee is helping make a delicious food for us to eat.

You know one of the foods that bees make. *Honey.*

When we think of bees, we think of honey. But it isn't honey that the bees are making here.

They haven't started making it yet. They are only gathering a sweet juice called *nectar* to take back to the hive, where other bees will make it into honey.

In gathering the nectar, these bees are actually helping make apples.

It doesn't sound reasonable, does it?

Well, here is the way it works. It starts with something called *pollen*.

Pollen looks like dust. It grows in a flower.

If pollen from one flower falls on a special part of another flower, something wonderful starts to happen. A fruit will begin to grow!

Such fruits as apples, oranges, pears, and peaches grow when the right pollen for each fruit reaches just the right flower. And that's where the honeybee comes in.

When a bee crawls around inside a flower, pollen sticks to the bee's fuzzy legs. Later, when the bee is crawling around inside another flower, some specks of the pollen may rub off onto just the right part of the flower. And then the fruit will start growing.

The bee doesn't know it's being so helpful. But without bees to move the pollen, there wouldn't be so much good fruit to eat.

Soon after some of the pollen falls on the special place in the flower, the petals drop off and the rest of the flower begins to change.

In a few weeks a tiny fruit is formed.

And a few weeks later the fruit is big and ripe and ready to eat.

What Kind of Bug Is This?

If you answer, "A ladybug," you are right about its nickname. (It is also known as a ladybird beetle.) And you may know a little verse about it—

Ladybug, ladybug,
Fly away home. . . .

But the ladybug isn't a true bug. Not every creeping, crawling, wriggling, flying creature is a bug, as many people think. Bugs are only part of a big group of little creatures called *insects*. For example, a ladybug doesn't have thickened front wings folded over its back the way true bugs have. And it doesn't have the long, beaky mouthparts for sucking the juices of plants.

There are many different kinds of insects. They may be as tiny as a dot or as big as a mouse. They may be long or short, fat or slim, black or brightly colored. Some insects fly, some crawl, some hop.

But in some ways all full-grown insects are alike. The easiest way to know an insect is to count its legs. All insects have six legs —three pairs.

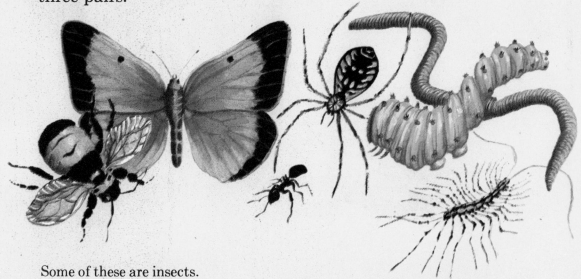

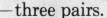
Some of these are insects.

Insects have bodies with three parts—
a head with a pair of feelers, or *antennas;*
a middle part, called *thorax,* with legs and usually wings growing from it;
a hind part, called *abdomen.*

All insects, like the dragonfly above, have a shell-like covering that they shed from time to time as they grow.

Insects have many different habits.

Bee
Makes honey

Butterfly
Flies south
in late summer

Cricket
First summer
concert singer

Walks upside down
on the ceiling

Doodlebug
Walks backward in circles

Water Strider
Skates on the water

Mosquito
The ladies sing and sting

Cicada
Sleeps for 17 years

Firefly
Flashes a light

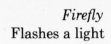

Mantis
Can look over its shoulder

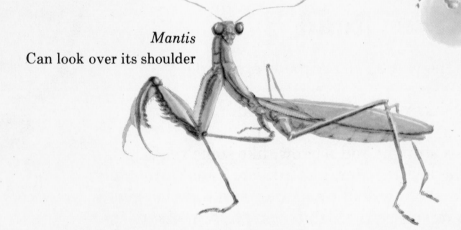

A caterpillar is an insect, too. It doesn't look like an insect, but it will after it turns into a butterfly. Now when you look at this picture, you know why the ant, the butterfly, the bee, and the caterpillar are insects. The earthworm isn't an insect. It doesn't have *any* legs. And the centipede has *too many* legs! Why isn't the spider an insect?

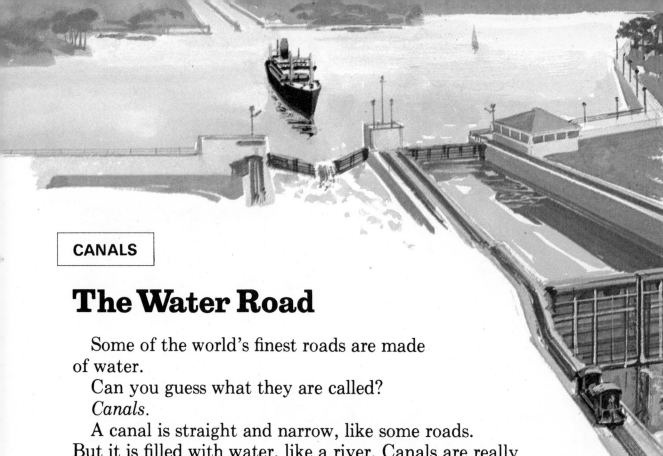

The Water Road

Some of the world's finest roads are made of water.

Can you guess what they are called?

Canals.

A canal is straight and narrow, like some roads. But it is filled with water, like a river. Canals are really water roads that are dug by men to join together rivers or lakes or oceans so that boats can go from one to the other.

On the canals the boats often have to be pulled along. In olden days, horses or mules walking on a towpath beside a canal pulled the boats. Today the boats are often pulled by electric locomotives. Sometimes the locomotives are called *electric mules*.

Canals even go over hills and mountains.

But you know that water can't flow *up* a hill—so how can the water and boats in a canal go up a hill?

Something called a *lock* is used. Not the kind of lock you have on your door. A different kind of lock. It is really a giant tank—a tank big enough to hold a whole long boat.

The boat floats into the tank, and doors are closed behind it to lock it in there. Then more water is let into the tank.

When the tank is full of water, the tank door in front of the boat is opened, and the boat floats out. The boat floats higher and higher as the water rises. It floats either out into a higher part of the canal or into another tank, or lock, which will lift it still higher.

To go down the hill on the other side, the boat enters a lock that is full of water. As the water is let *out* of the lock, the boat floats lower and lower.

To see how a boat goes up and down in a canal tank, or lock, do this:

Put a cork in a glass and then slowly fill the glass with water. The cork rises to the top of the glass. If you pour the water out, the cork goes down. The boat does the same thing in the canal lock when water is let in or let out. And that is how a boat can go up or down a hill.

There is a city named Venice
where many of the streets are
canals. Houses and beautiful
churches and hotels look as if
they are floating in the water. In
some places there is not even
room at the sides of the canals
for a towpath or a sidewalk—the
water touches the sides of the
houses. If you were in Venice and
wanted to go somewhere, you
might step out of your door into
a boat. Some of the boats are
gondolas—strange-looking boats,
high at each end. A man stands
at the back of the gondola and
moves a long oar back and forth
to make the gondola go.

The Tiger in Your House

Is this a wild jungle tiger about to jump out of the page and eat somebody?

No. It is a cuddly, soft kitten playing in someone's house.

But a tiger is a cat. So is a lion, a leopard, a cheetah, a jaguar, a lynx, a panther, and a puma. They are all cats.

All of them leap and run and pounce and snarl.

Many climb trees.

Many purr and meow.

Many don't like to go in water.

They can see better at night than people can.

They are among the fastest of furred animals.

They have five toes on their front paws and four on their back paws. And probably you have found out that cats have long, sharp claws. They use their claws for climbing trees, catching food, and protecting themselves against other animals. The claws in the front toes of most cats can be moved in and out. Now you see them, and now you don't.

Yes, your soft, playful kitty and the lion, leopard, and tiger are all cats. But not all cats are pet cats. Not all cats are the kind of cats you would want to put your arms around and cuddle.

A new baby lion is so small that you could hold it in your arms. But lions grow very fast. A baby lion would soon be big enough to hold *you* in its arms.

There have been cats on the Earth for a very, very long time. Much longer than dogs and wolves and bears.

As far back as caveman days, there were wildcats prowling the woods. Cavemen probably tamed some of the smaller cats and let them live in the caves, where they could chase away the rats and mice and snakes that tried to get in.

One cat called the *saber-toothed tiger* was *not* a pet. It was as big as some automobiles of today. Cavemen scared these cats away with fires they kept burning at night.

Long ago in the country of Egypt, the people thought that cats were magic. The Egyptian people made statues of cats out of wood and stone. Milk for the cats was sometimes put in saucers of gold. When cats died, they were buried in special cat graveyards.

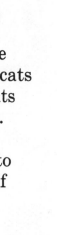

In another country—once called Siam—cats lived in the castles with the kings. Some cats were trained to be warrior cats and to guard the castle walls. Siamese cats have very loud voices. They were supposed to yowl and screech a warning if enemies came near.

Sea captains of the old-time sailing ships brought Siamese cats home to their children, and now these blue-eyed cats are nearly everywhere. Perhaps you have seen them. When they are kittens, they have soft, white fur, with a dark nose and tail and dark ears and paws.

Today for pets we have short-haired cats and long-haired cats, as well as bobtail, calico, Maltese, tiger, tabby, and many other kinds of cats. Cats are among the smartest of all tame animals. They can do tricks— open doors and ring doorbells. But lots of times they don't want to. It is hard to teach them tricks, because they don't like to be bossed. They like to have their own way.

You may have heard people say that cats have nine lives. They don't, really. But they are so quick and so surefooted that they may escape danger many times in their lives.

67

What Are Plants and Animals Made Of?

The four things in the blue circle don't look the same. They have different shapes and different sizes. The two bigger ones are animals and the other two are plants.

But all the things in this picture can be called by the same name —*cell*. Most plants and animals that have only one cell are very, very tiny—so small that they can be seen only under a microscope.

A few special cells are large enough to be seen without a microscope—like the cell of a chicken egg that holds the yolk and a tiny spot that will grow and become a chicken. The clear part and the shell aren't part of the cell—they protect it.

Most plants and animals that can be seen without a microscope have thousands or millions of cells. These cells make the plant or animal look and act the way it does.

Different cells do different jobs inside our bodies. We have

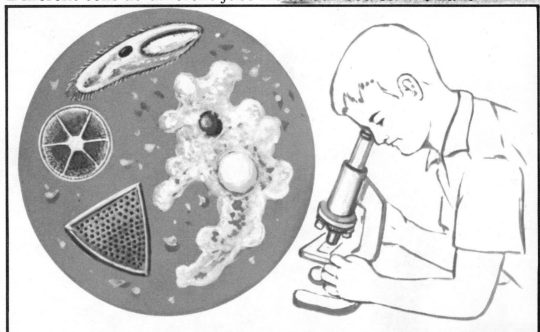

muscle cells and nerve cells and blood cells and skin cells. Plants
have leaf cells and root cells and flower cells—cells of many kinds.
Every living thing you can name is made up of one kind of cell or
another.

The Riddle Tree

If a tree could speak in riddles, this tall evergreen tree might say—

"My branches are not good for climbing or for swinging.

"The blossoms that bloom among my leaves are not very fragrant, and my seeds are bitter. But children like me.

"What kind of tree am I?"

Did you guess that this is a chocolate tree? That doesn't mean it is made out of chocolate—not even its bark, which is the color of chocolate. And chocolate syrup will not drip out of its trunk if someone taps a hole in it. But this tree does grow chocolate.

The chocolate is in the pods that grow out of its trunk.

Inside the pods are rows of seeds called
cocoa beans. Each is about the size and
shape of a big fingernail. It is from these
cocoa beans that we get one of the world's
favorite flavors—chocolate.

The cocoa bean tree grows only in very
hot, wet countries, but luckily the beans
can be shipped easily to places all over the
world. Then, in chocolate factories, the
beans are roasted and ground into a thick
syrup.

Taste it. *Ugh*—it's bitter.

But after it is mixed with sugar and
other tasty things, it is used in many
delicious drinks and candies and
desserts that we know about.

Rocks That Burn

"They're nothing but rocks—black rocks!"

"That man's trying to cheat us."

"He's trying to sell us rocks——"

"All right," the man said, "call them rocks if you want to, but they're 'rocks' that burn. They'll heat your houses in the winter, and they'll make steam to run the machines in your mills and factories."

This kind of talk happened a long time ago in city markets when men tried to sell a new kind of very hard coal that had just been discovered. People wouldn't buy the coal at first. They thought the men were trying to sell rocks, and everybody knows that rocks won't burn in a fireplace or a stove or anywhere else.

A piece of coal does look like a rock and has been called a rock that burns. But coal really isn't rock. At one time it was a tree or parts of many, many trees.

How can trees change into something that looks like a rock?

Well, millions of years ago there were great, hot, swampy jungles in the world. The trees grew in water and spongy soil, so close together that it would have been hard to tell where one tree started and another ended. Grasses and ferns grew as tall as some of the strange-looking trees.

When the growing things died or the wind blew them down, they partly decayed in the warm mud, and more trees and grasses grew in their place. Finally all this material decayed and became what is called *peat*.

This kept happening for more years than you could count. Rivers, lakes, and seas washed sand and soil on top of everything. Earthquakes shook the land and covered some of it still deeper.

Under all that weight of land the peat was slowly . . . slowly . . . slowly squashed so tightly together that it turned into coal.

This coal is burned today to heat houses and to help make the steam and electricity that run factory machinery.

But most of this coal is formed deep under the ground. How do we get it out?

Some of the coal is close enough to the top of the ground to be *strip-mined*. This means that giant shovels—shovels as high as a house and run by machinery—move along the top of the ground and *strip,* or shovel off, the dirt and rocks from above the layer of coal. After the coal is uncovered, it is broken up and loaded onto trucks or railroad cars.

When coal is deep down, tunnels or shafts are dug into the ground to reach it. In some places the coal is then brought out of the mine on long *conveyor belts* that keep moving the way an escalator does. In other mines the coal is hoisted up the shaft in *cages,* or elevators.

But first the miners go down the hole, or mine shaft, in a cage. They go down and down into darkness, but when they step out on the bottom of the coal mine, they step into brightness. Electric lights make everything look a little like a small city at night. Offices and machine shops have been hollowed out of the coal. These are on broad "streets," or tunnels, where tracks for the little coal-mine trains run in every direction.

To get to their working places, the miners ride in the empty coal cars far into the mine, where it is so dark that they have to carry lights with them. Most of the train tunnels are so narrow that the miners can reach out and touch the rough walls as the coal trains roar along.

For many years drills and black powder explosives were used to break up the coal so that it could be handled with a pick and shovel. Today coal-cutting machinery and machine loaders are used. After the coal has been put into the coal cars, it is taken to the mine opening, where it is removed and dumped into big railroad cars.

Coal has been called buried sunlight because of all the sunlight it took to grow the trees that later became coal. But there is no sunlight in a coal mine. Almost everything in a coal mine is black or hard or sharp or heavy.

Air is pumped into a mine for the miners to breathe. But sometimes the air doesn't move as it is supposed to, and different kinds of gas may collect. The gas can cause an explosion, or it can make the air unfit to breathe. Water can flood a mine. The coal can catch fire and fill the mine with smoke. Slate and rock can fall on the miners' heads. The coal cars sometimes run off the track. There is really no safe place in a coal mine. But the men who run the mines are always looking for safer ways to dig the coal.

The Big Lizards

If you see a long, mossy-green log floating in the water, look carefully. It might not be a log. If you are in a hot, wet country, it might be a crocodile or an alligator.

Neither of these animals can breathe underwater, as a fish does, but each can hold its breath and swim underwater for a long time. Both have tough, thick skins to protect them from enemies, and a big mouthful of very sharp teeth.

76

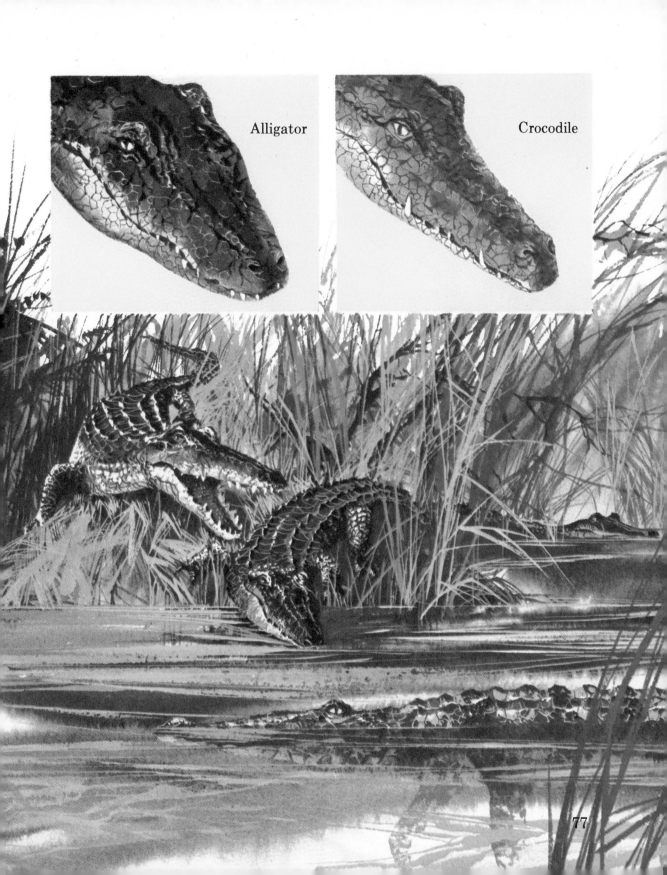

Alligator

Crocodile

To many people a crocodile and an alligator look alike. But in some ways they are different, as the pictures show. Here is a rhyme about them.

While sailing down the river Nile,
I chanced upon a crocodile.
I knew him by his narrow nose,
His great long head, and scaly "clothes."

Far away and some time later,
I sailed up to an alligator.
Though shorter than the crocodile,
He seemed to stretch about a mile!

78

Now, both these reptiles swim with skill.
And both of them will bite and kill!
Both have teeth as sharp as nails,
Snapping jaws, and slapping tails.

They run quite fast on short, squat legs.
In sand and mud they lay their eggs.
And soon the small ones can be seen,
So tiny—but they grow up mean!

If you should ever have to go
Where these monsters live and grow,
I think you'd better watch them float
From the safety of a boat.

They Take Their Homes with Them

Fill 'er up!

These people, getting ready to travel across the desert to look for a new place to live, must water their camels. The camel driver tries to get each camel to drink as much water as possible because the little water that these people take along they will need themselves.

A very big camel can hold more water than some cars can hold gasoline! That's why the camel can go for many days without having to drink. It's a good thing that the camel can do this, because it may have to in the great, dry desert.

Nomads never keep their homes in one place very long. They're always moving. That's what nomads are—people who wander around instead of living in one place.

Every time the Arab nomads set out across the hot, sandy desert, it is a new adventure. They must find food for the animals, or the animals will die.

A sudden windstorm sometimes forces the nomads to stop in the middle of their search. They pull their heavy wool hoods over their faces and make the camels lie down. Then they hide behind the camels, away from the biting sand. The tougher bodies of their camels can take the blowing sand much better than their own bodies can.

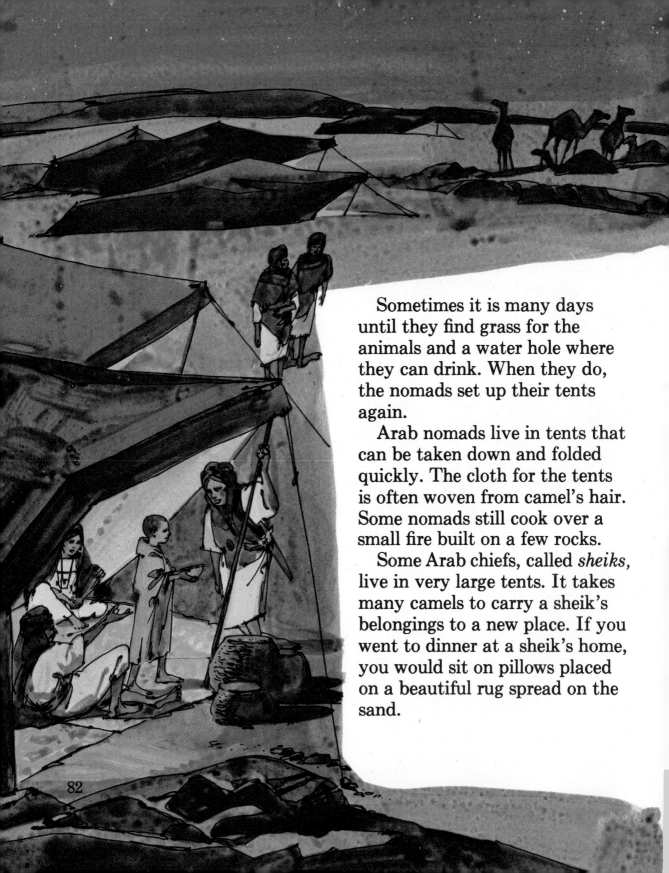

Sometimes it is many days until they find grass for the animals and a water hole where they can drink. When they do, the nomads set up their tents again.

Arab nomads live in tents that can be taken down and folded quickly. The cloth for the tents is often woven from camel's hair. Some nomads still cook over a small fire built on a few rocks.

Some Arab chiefs, called *sheiks*, live in very large tents. It takes many camels to carry a sheik's belongings to a new place. If you went to dinner at a sheik's home, you would sit on pillows placed on a beautiful rug spread on the sand.

All nomads aren't Arabs, of course, and there are nomads who don't live on deserts.

In countries where there are many big cities, no one *needs* to be a nomad. Still, there are many people who like the changing life of a nomad.

Gypsies used to travel in carts—stopping now and then to trade or to buy or sell horses. They also made small things to sell, told fortunes, played music, and danced under the moon. Today many Gypsies travel in cars or trailers.

There will always be some people who like to move around and to see and live in new places. Some people live in a trailer. Whenever they want to move to a new place, they hook up their truck or automobile to their trailer and away they go. Sailors on ships might be called water nomads.

The Most Valuable Stones in the World

They sparkle and glitter in the light. No other rocks are so hard. They are very valuable. It might cost thousands and thousands of dollars to buy just one. Most are found in the ground. The largest one ever discovered is as big as a man's fist. But most are tiny.

They're diamonds!

For hundreds of years men have risked their lives searching for diamonds. To many the discovery of this glittering treasure has seemed more important than the discovery of new lands. Fairy stories tell of brave knights who battled fierce dragons and evil wizards to win kingdoms rich with diamonds.

In the Tower of London in England, there is a very special room protected by guards. There, inside a thick glass case, are jeweled crowns once worn by kings and queens. People from all over the world come to see the shimmering diamonds and other precious stones that shine from behind the glass.

Most diamonds seem to flash with a kind of white fire. But there are diamonds that sparkle in other colors, too. Sometimes diamonds are discovered in gravel at the bottom of rivers and streams. (To get these diamonds, the gravel is sucked up through giant hoses that act like vacuum cleaners.) Diamonds are found in rivers, on land, and in great stretches of hot desert sand. A few small ones are even found in or near meteorites that strike the ground from outer space.

But most diamonds are found in rocks deep inside the diamond mines of Africa. The diamonds were made millions and millions of years ago when flaming volcanoes melted a mineral called *carbon*, which was a part of these rocks. Gigantic earthquakes shook the rocks and pressed them tightly together. The hot melted carbon in the rocks was squeezed at the same time—squeezed so tightly that by the time it cooled, it had changed into the lovely hard gems called *diamonds*.

85

To get at these valuable diamond rocks, workers ride in an elevator that goes down and down into the blackness far below the ground. Tunnels connect this deep shaft with the openings—called *pipes*—inside the ancient volcanoes.

When they are first dug from the mines, diamonds don't glitter or sparkle as they do when we see them in rings or other jewelry. They look more like dull bits of glass. A man who knows all about diamonds—a diamond cutter—must cut them just right. Diamonds are so hard that nothing can cut them except the edge of another diamond.

Using his diamond-edged tools, the diamond cutter carefully removes tiny pieces so that the diamond will have many sharp edges and smooth surfaces—like little windows. It is because of these sharp edges and smooth surfaces that the diamond reflects light, sparkles and flashes with tiny bursts of color, and seems almost ablaze with fire. Diamond cutters often use diamond saws. The fine powder—diamond dust—that is left after the sawing is done can be used in a kind of sandpaper to polish the sparkling gems.

Not all diamonds are clear enough or pretty enough or large enough to be made into jewelry. But because they are so hard, they can be used for other things, such as points for drills, pen tips, and needles for record players. These diamonds are called *industrial diamonds*. Some of them are man made. Carbon is heated until it is very hot and then squeezed. If men ever learn how to make it hot enough and to squeeze it tightly enough, they will probably be able to make big diamonds. Then maybe diamonds will be cheap enough to use as buttons on your shirt or coat!

Pterodactyl

Brontosaur

Stegosaur

Monsters of the Past

They were the biggest, scariest creatures that ever lived. The word *dinosaur* means "terrible lizard." Which one of these do you think was the most terrible?

Brontosaur. The "thunder lizard" weighed as much as ten elephants and probably sounded like thunder when it walked. But it ate only plants—never touched a bit of meat.

Pterodactyl. It'd even scare a witch on a broomstick! This "wing-fingered" dinosaur swooped across the sky like a dragon kite.

Tyrannosaur

Trachodon

Triceratops

Stegosaur. This one was covered with hard, bony plates from head to tail. And when it wagged that tail, it wasn't being friendly. The tail had four long spikes at the tip.

Tyrannosaur. This dinosaur, known as the "king of the lizards," was as long as a fire truck. The teeth in its jaws were like big knives.

Trachodon. This terrible duck-billed lizard had 2,000 teeth!

Triceratops. This "three-horned" lizard looked like an army tank and was just as unfriendly.

There were many other kinds of dinosaurs. They lived almost everywhere. The very land beneath your bedroom may once have throbbed and thundered to the tread of these huge creatures.

What if dinosaurs were still alive?

How impatient you'd be if a dinosaur were in your way as you tried to cross the street!

How surprised you'd be if you awoke one night to see a dinosaur peering in your upstairs bedroom window!

How little food there'd be for you to eat if you had to share it with a dinosaur! Some of them ate more food in *one day* than you eat in a whole year.

You don't have to worry about any of this happening, of course, because dinosaurs completely disappeared from the Earth so long ago that it is hard to think back that far.

How do we know that once upon a time there were dinosaurs? Because we keep finding their bones.

Let's pretend we are living in dinosaur days, when the air was hot and thick and heavy, and there was water here and there and everywhere because it rained so much. And here we are, hidden behind the leaves of the topmost branch of a tree that grows by a muddy pond. We see that the enormous log near the edge of the pond is not a log at all. It is a duck-billed dinosaur that has been taking a nap. Now it's getting up! It's clambering out of the water and heading toward our tree!

The duckbill rips the leaves from a branch that's almost touching the one on which we're hiding. Now it lowers its head, munching the leaves. It swallows them in one gulp. *Rip!* There go the leaves on a branch that's even closer to us.

Suddenly, high above the treetops, we see the head of a dinosaur that is even taller and uglier than the first one. We know from its great size and the hooklike claws on its short front feet that this is the kind of dinosaur called "king of the lizards," the most dangerous beast on Earth.

Its mouth opens and closes like a giant pair of scissors. Terrible cries tear across the sky as the "king of the lizards" starts after the duckbill. When the fight is over, the duck-billed dinosaur is dead. After eating as much of the duckbill as it can, the lizard king waddles away to find a quiet place to sleep until it is hungry again.

The bones of the duckbill lie at the edge of the pond.

It begins to rain, and the rain washes the bones over the edge of the pond into the water.

More rains come and wash dirt from the bank of the pond. The dirt settles as mud over the bones. This happens for millions of years.

Slowly, as millions of more years go by, the weather changes. There is little or no rain. The sun is bright. It shines everywhere because there is no shade. The grass and trees have dried up and blown away in hot winds. The mud that surrounded the duckbill bones is dry now, too, and nearly as hard as rock. The duckbill is buried under an almost empty desert.

Who knows? Maybe nobody will ever find its bones. But maybe they will. Some day an explorer (maybe you!) might come along, looking for dinosaur bones. He might dig in just the right place and find them. What a wonderful discovery!

It has happened before. It has happened many times. And today in the museums of big cities, you can see these bones put together as they were when they were part of real dinosaurs many millions of years ago.

Courtesy Field Museum of Natural History, Chicago

Champion Swimmers

What's going on here? We can see a feathered tail and a big webbed foot.

No head! No neck!

What's going on?

It's a duck poking its long beak into the muddy bottom of a stream to find food—an insect, or perhaps a shellfish hidden down there.

Ducks are at home almost anywhere near water. Some feed and nest in streams and ponds. Others live near deep, wide lakes. Some make their homes on rocky cliffs by the ocean.

The ducks on this page don't
stand on their heads to get food.
They dive straight down into a
lake or ocean to snap up fish and
water plants. They can stay
under water for a long time.

Ducks are champion swimmers.
And they fly high and gracefully
over mountains and tall buildings. But on the ground? With
feet that seem too big for their
bodies, they waddle from side to
side, moving slowly in a funny,
jerky way!

Even though ducks usually fly south in the wintertime, the
iciest water doesn't seem too cold for them. A thick coat of
feathers keeps them warm. And it's waterproof. Feathers are a
duck's raincoat!

The tiniest, fluffiest duck feathers—called *down*—are used to
line the nest and keep the eggs warm when the mother duck is
away.

Most nests are built in hollows near the water. But many are
attached to the tall stalks that grow over marshy ponds. Some
ducks even look for holes in the tops of trees to make nests for
their eggs.

Baby ducklings don't need to *learn* how to swim. They *know!*
The minute these soft, downy baby birds waddle out of the nest,
they head for the water.

And here's a strange thing. As soon as their babies are hatched,
the grown-up ducks start losing their feathers. Until new feathery
coats are grown, the ducks can't fly. So they hide in the grasses
along the shore to keep safe from enemies.

They fly, they waddle.
They swim with ease.
They build their nests in stalks and trees.
On land, in lakes,
Or high in the air,
Ducks live almost anywhere!

Riders of the Wind

If this eagle spread its wings in your room, it would take up as much space as your bed. Yet this heavy bird flies easily, sometimes using air currents to ride the wind.

Eagles build huge nests of sticks (big enough to hold people!) on rocky cliffs and use the same nest year after year.

When there are eggs to hatch, both the mother and father eagles take turns sitting on them. And both parents care for the little eagles afterward, bringing them mice, fish, rabbits, ducks, snakes, or squirrels to eat. But eagles don't always catch their own food. Sometimes they steal it from another bird by chasing it high in the sky until the tired bird drops the food it is carrying in its beak.

You would expect such a big bird to make a big sound. But the eagle's sound is a kind of squealing, not nearly so loud and fierce as you'd expect.

If an eagle has to protect itself, it uses its hooked beak and strong claws. Its claws can go through the toughest skin.

This bird has very good eyesight, too. Even when it is so high in the air that it can hardly be seen, the eagle can see small things on the ground.

Eagles do not all look alike. A golden eagle wears a cap of gold feathers. A bald eagle is not really bald. It looks that way because its head feathers are white. Some eagles have "boots" of feathers all the way down to their claws. Others have just plain naked legs.

Pictures of eagles appear on coins and seals. But real eagles are getting scarce, and now there are laws to save the ones that are left.

Inside the Earth

What is the boy in this picture sitting on?

He's sitting on a *chair*. But that's not all he's sitting on. Under the chair is a *rug*. Under the rug is a *floor*. Under the floor is a *cellar*. Under the cellar is the *ground*.

But that's not all!

Under the ground that is under the cellar that is under the floor that is under the rug that is under the chair that is under the boy is the rest of the Earth.

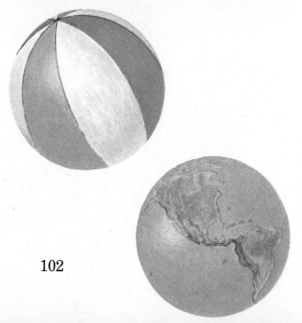

We know what the outside of the Earth looks like. From far out in space it looks something like a ball. No one has ever had a chance to look very far *inside* the Earth. But we think we know some of the things we would find if we could.

If the inside of the Earth really is the way these scientists think it is—and if it could be sliced like a melon or a peach—it would look like this.

Most scientists believe that the Earth is filled with layers of rock, one on top of another. In the center, or middle, there is probably a ball—or *core*— of metal that is mostly iron.

The deepest hole we have been able to dig into our very solid Earth is two miles deep.

A hole that would show us for sure what's in the very middle of the Earth would have to be about 4,000 miles deep.

Our two-mile-deep holes have proved *something*. They have proved that the deeper we dig or drill a hole, *the hotter it gets*. The temperature at the bottom of a two-mile hole is hot enough to boil water. Deeper down, the Earth is still hotter. It is so hot that if we went far enough, the tools that were doing the digging would melt!

Because the inside of the Earth is so hot, we'll probably never learn about it by drilling holes. Fortunately, there are other ways to learn.

A *volcano* looks like a mountain stuffed with exploding fireworks. It shoots out fire and smoke and rocks. Some of the rocks inside the volcano are so hot that they melt. This melted rock, or *lava*, runs out like thick chocolate and spreads all around. After the lava has cooled, scientists can learn a lot about what's inside the Earth by looking carefully at the melted rock that poured out of the volcano.

There is still another way to learn about what's inside the Earth.

Sometimes a big layer of rock that is deep, deep down slips and rubs against another layer of rock. This causes a shaking and rumbling called an *earthquake*.

Scientists learn something about what's inside the Earth by using special earthquake instruments.

What's inside the Earth is a riddle. Nature gives us some hints when volcanoes shoot out melted rock and when there are earthquakes. It lets us know that in some places there is solid rock, and in other places hot melted rock, and in still other places hot melted iron. But we still need to know a lot more than we do. When you grow up, you might be the one who will tell us exactly what is under the ground that is under the cellar that is under the floor that is under the rug that is under the chair where the boy is sitting!

The Sky's Greatest Show

Once upon a time—so the story goes—an explorer was captured by a tribe of natives in the jungle. The jungle people had no books or television or radio. They didn't even know that there was anything different in the world from the trees and the vines and the muddy rivers of their jungle. They were afraid of the explorer, and so they locked him up in a wooden cage.

"Let me out," the explorer said, "or I'll make the sun go away. Right here in the middle of the day I'll make something in the sky eat up your sun."

The jungle people didn't believe him. They laughed and poked sticks at him through the bars of the cage.

"All right," he said, "you'll see. My magic is strong. Now I'll make the sun go away in the middle of the day."

And the sun did go away! At least it seemed to. Something seemed to eat up the sun a little at a time until it was all gone, and the day was as dark as midnight.

The jungle people moaned and cried. They were very much afraid of this explorer whose magic was strong enough to take their sun away.

"Make the sun come back," they cried, "and we'll do anything you say. We'll set you free and give you food and great treasure."

"All right," the explorer said, "I'll make the sun come back."

And the sun did come back after a little while.

Do you know why it "went away" in the first place? And why it "came back"?

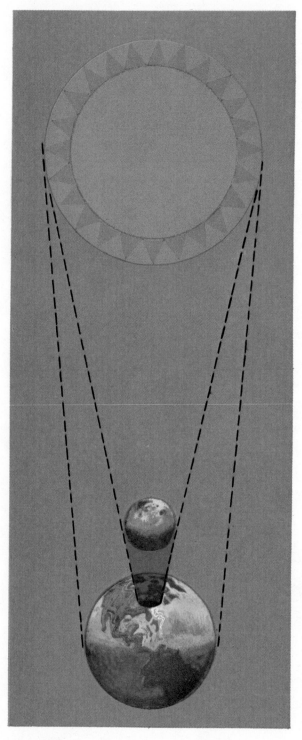

It really can turn as dark as night—right in the middle of the day. This happens when the sun is *eclipsed* by the moon. *Eclipse* means to hide something by coming in front of it.

You know that the moon goes around the Earth. And that the Earth and moon together go around the sun. Once in a while, as they all move, the moon gets between the sun and the Earth. That stops the sun's light from reaching part of the Earth. It gets dark in the daytime, and we say that there is an eclipse of the sun.

Scientists who study the sky can tell when these eclipses will happen. The explorer in our story knew there would be an eclipse. So he pretended to the jungle people that *he* made it happen.

When the moon comes between the sun and the Earth, the sun looks thinner and thinner until— almost as if somebody flicked off a light switch—the day becomes as dark as night. Even the animals are fooled. Birds stop singing, and hens go clucking to their roosts, thinking it is time to sleep.

Eclipses of the moon also happen but in a different way.

When the Earth gets in front of the sun, it throws a long black shadow over the moon. But some sunlight "leaks" through to the moon; so it never turns black, only a dull coppery color.

Eclipses of the sun or the moon don't happen often. The next time the sun is eclipsed where you live and it suddenly gets dark, don't be fooled and go to bed in the middle of the day like the chickens.

Even though the sun is darkened during an eclipse, never stare at it. There are still enough harmful rays to hurt your eyes.

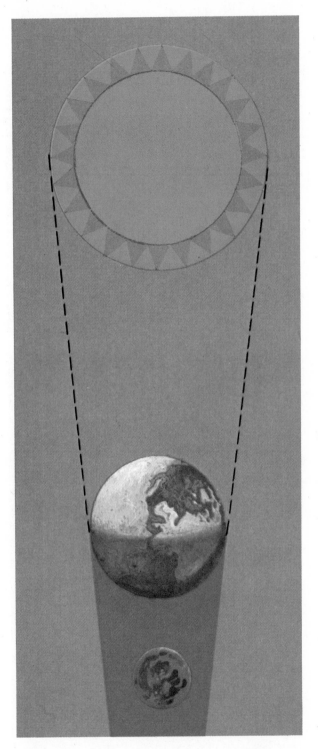

What's Inside?

When we think of eggs, we usually think of birds' eggs. But such animals as lizards and salamanders also come from eggs.

Or an egg may have a snake inside.

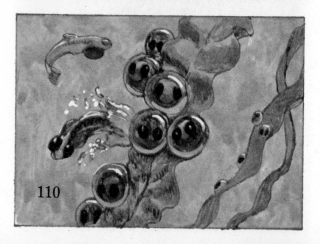

Many fish start out in eggs, too—in tiny eggs without hard shells.

Some eggs are so small that you wouldn't know they were there unless you had a magnifying glass.

110

This mother fish is a *perch*.

And on these strips of jelly—her underwater nest—are hundreds and hundreds of tiny eggs. A tiny piece of her nest could hold as many eggs as there are grains in a heaping tablespoonful of sugar.

Even baby dinosaurs poked and pushed their way out of eggs. These creatures lived millions of years ago and were the largest animals ever to walk on Earth— yet some of them were born from eggs not much larger than a cucumber! Some of the eggs were round like circles and were laid in nests that were built in the sand. The shells of the eggs felt almost like leather.

Not very long ago, scientists made a famous discovery of dinosaur eggs in the Gobi Desert in Mongolia in Asia. The eggs they found had the bones of unhatched dinosaurs inside.

It is believed that certain furry animals may have eaten dinosaur eggs millions of years ago and that this is one reason there aren't any dinosaurs anymore.

These aren't dinosaur eggs. They're robin eggs. The warm body of the mother robin covers each egg when she sits on the nest. If the eggs are not kept warm, the baby birds growing inside will die. So the mother bird sits and sits and sits.

One day she feels a bump. Then come stronger bumps . . . and still stronger *bumps* . . . until there's a BUMP that almost pushes the mother bird out of the nest. Now this is what she sees.

At first there's just a crack, going this way and that. Then the crack in the egg widens into a hole—not a smooth, round one but an every-which-way hole. A busy little beak, pecking and pushing, makes the hole grow and *grow* and GROW.

And then, at last, the baby bird is out of its shell.

Some eggs are as blue as the sky.

Others are as pink as a sunset.

Still others are speckled and freckled with color.

Some birds lay their eggs on the ground. Often these eggs match the colors of the ground so that other hungry animals won't find them.

When an animal comes out of its egg, it may be protected and fed by its parents for a while, but soon it will leave their protection. It, too, will become a parent and have eggs of its own to care for.

The Highest Climb

Each day the men climbed higher on the icy mountain cliffs. Finally, they reached a narrow shelf of rock, where most of the tired party stopped to rest. But two men continued to climb from this high camp.

The slippery rock made each step seem more difficult than the one before. In some places the two men had to cling to the steep rock like ants on a wall. The cold wind bit at their eyes and tugged at their clothes. It threatened to pull them loose from the mountain—to send them falling against the rock a thousand feet below.

The air was so thin that the two men had to breathe from tanks of oxygen strapped to their backs. They became so tired and cold that they could barely move.

They looked back down the icy slope . . . down . . . down to the black storm clouds. They were high above the clouds!

They started climbing toward the top again. Would they make it? Everyone who had tried before had failed. Many had been killed trying to climb to the windy, snow-covered top of this high mountain.

Slowly, steadily, they kept climbing until they reached the last icy cliff. They knew they were close to the top. But how close? Blinding, swirling snow kept them from seeing.

They kept climbing anyway. They had to chop places in the ice for their hands and feet. They kept on, blindly, until finally when they reached to feel the rock ahead, there was no rock. They knew then that they had reached the top.

It was on May 29, 1953, that Edmund Hillary and Tenzing Norgay reached the top of Mount Everest, the highest mountain in the world. They were the first men ever to do this. Mount Everest is in the Himalayan Mountains between India and China.

Time to Wake Up, Everybody

When the summer sun comes up and the green grass waits to tickle your toes and the rooster crows—

That's a good time to visit the farm animals.

Most chickens these days are raised on special chicken farms. But not all chickens are.

Cock-a-doodle-doo!

The red comb of the rooster quivers as he beats his wings.

Cock-a-doodle-doo! He's telling everybody it's time to get up.

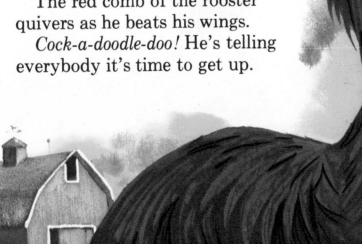

Chickens and turkeys uncurl their toes from around perching places. They have long toes for holding onto sticks or branches. They use the sharp claws in their toes to scratch for bugs and worms. They also eat corn, oats, and wheat, snipping up their food with pointed beaks.

Feathered animals don't have teeth. They don't chew their food. They swallow little stones, which help grind their food.

The ducks and geese awake, too. Sometimes they eat what chickens and turkeys eat, but their beaks are flatter and rounder and longer—good for digging in mud and for scooping up water bugs. Their feet are like swim fins—good for paddling. Because their feathers are oily, water does not soak into them and make them heavy. Their oily feathers keep them from drowning when they swim in the pond.

The feathered animals raise their babies from eggs. A mother hen sits on her eggs and keeps them warm. The baby bird grows inside the shell. Then one day it pecks its way out. Soon the warm air dries the wet chick into a bundle of fluff.

And look—the baby chick's eyes are on the sides of its head. It can see all around. It's hard for an enemy to sneak up on it.

Look who else the rooster has awakened. This fat sow's babies— curly-tailed pigs with short legs and silky hair. (Their hair will

become stiff and scratchy when they grow up.) Pigs have snouts at the end of their faces. They can poke their snouts into the ground to find vegetables and roots to eat. Pigs like corn and oats, too. But they will eat almost anything. (The father pig, the *boar,* eats most of all and grows very big.) And all pigs like to rest in mud puddles to cool their thick skin.

Now look who's awake in the big, green pasture. Cows, with their fly-swatter tails. Cows can live all summer on grass if they have water to drink and a block of salt to lick.

Cows can't bite off grass because they have no teeth in the top front of their mouths. They tear it off. The grass is swallowed into their *first* stomachs. Later, the grass comes back up into their mouths to be chewed like a big wad of gum, and then it slides into their *second* stomachs! Chewing their food a second time is called *chewing their cud*.

When a calf is born, the mother licks its face. Sometimes this opens its nose and helps the calf start breathing. Then the mother washes the calf with her tongue. If the calf doesn't get right up on its wobbly legs, she nudges it with her head.

After some milk and a nap the calf is soon running around.

Don't go close to the calf's father, the *bull*. He'll probably chase you out of his pasture!

And look who's hard at work in the pasture. The farm dog wants the sheep to go through the gate. The sheep don't seem to understand. And the lambs don't seem to care.

Baby lambs are very active. They can jump higher than you can!

The father *ram*, the mother *ewe*, and the baby lambs all have soft, wavy hair. Sheep get "haircuts" all over. Their curly hair is the wool used to make clothes and blankets.

Sheep also have more than one stomach. A sheep has to chew its cud as cows do.

The goat is part of the sheep family. Some goats are woolly like sheep.

The nanny goat gives good-tasting milk. Her babies are called *kids*. Can you guess what the father is usually called? Billy goat!

Horses can run fast—even when carrying people.

A horse is so strong it can kick out the boards of a barn. It can pull a plow, a wagon, or almost any big farm machine. It eats corn, oats, hay, and other grains and grasses.

Its big mouth has many strong teeth. But if a horse likes you, it won't bite. Instead, it will nuzzle you with its nose and nip you with its soft lips, perhaps hoping for a sugar-cube treat. If ever you feed a horse sugar, hold your hand out flat so that your fingers won't accidentally get caught in its teeth!

Brushing makes a horse's long-haired tail and mane pretty. Sometimes its hooves have to be trimmed, just as the nails on your fingers and toes have to be trimmed.

A horse's hooves are hard, yet there is a soft spot on the bottom of its feet, where stones and thorns can stick. And its hooves

sometimes wear down and split. So most farm horses wear shoes. The shoes have to be fitted to their feet, just as your shoes do. But a horse's shoes are made of iron and are fastened on with nails. The nails don't hurt its hard hooves.

Some farms have mules instead of horses. A mule's mother is a horse, and its father is a donkey. Mules are very strong. They have long ears like their fathers.

All these animals live on farms. Can you think of any we missed seeing? Pigeons and sparrows? They usually stay around barns and fields to pick up dropped grain. Rats and mice? If you didn't see any, it's because of the barn cats.

Did you see the barn cats? Turn back and look for them.

125

The Blinking Bug

They blink a light—a softly glowing, golden green light. Or is it a golden red light? Or a golden blue light? It's hard to tell for sure.

They drift lazily in the warm summer night, over the grass and under the trees—just beyond your reaching fingers.

They look so invitingly easy to catch. But just about the time you think you have one, it floats silently away. It lifts or drops or zigs or zags—or its light goes out, and you can't see it at all.

You know what it is, don't you?

A firefly. Maybe you call it a lightning bug.

You *can* catch one if you keep trying. But hold it gently. Don't press hard with your fingers. Although it is a kind of beetle, it doesn't have a hard shell as so many other beetles have.

It is one of the nicest bugs you could ever catch. It doesn't bite or pinch or scratch. And its fire won't burn your hand. It looks hot, but it's not. The light of a lightning bug is *cold*.

Lightning bugs lay their eggs on the ground. When they hatch out, the baby lightning bugs burrow under the ground or hide in old, rotten stumps or logs.

There are many other kinds of lightning bugs besides the ones we see blinking and glowing on a summer evening. One, called the *glowworm,* doesn't fly at all. And there are lightning bugs so big that several in a glass jar make enough light that people in the jungle have used them to light their way on a dark jungle path.

Scientists think that the fireflies' blinking lights help the fireflies find each other and let the birds that eat at night know what kind of insects they are.

You might think that the fireflies would be safer if the birds didn't know. But this isn't true.

Most of the night-feeding birds do *not* like to eat fireflies. So, when they see the blinking lights, they leave the fireflies alone.

For years, scientists have been trying to find out how fireflies make their wonderful light. Some of the secret has been discovered. The scientists hope that someday they may be able to make this same kind of softly glowing light that never burns anybody. Then, perhaps, it will be used to light our homes and streets.

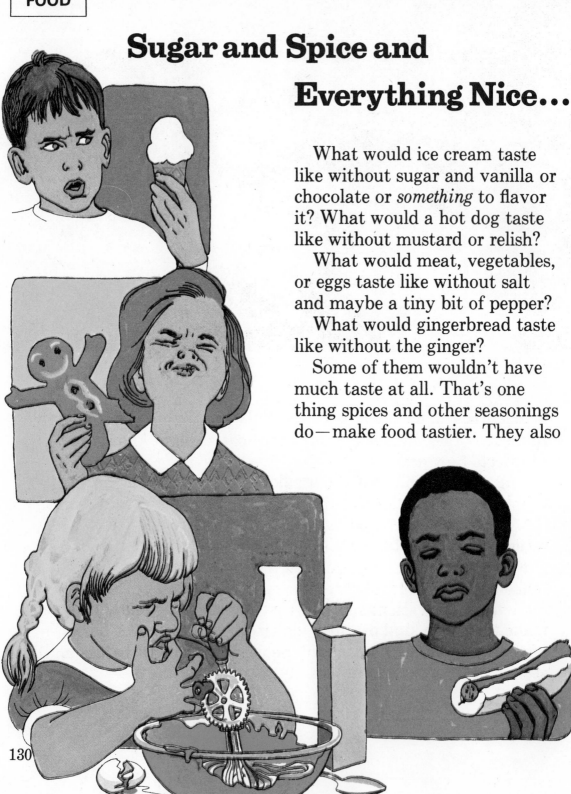

Sugar and Spice and Everything Nice...

What would ice cream taste like without sugar and vanilla or chocolate or *something* to flavor it? What would a hot dog taste like without mustard or relish?

What would meat, vegetables, or eggs taste like without salt and maybe a tiny bit of pepper?

What would gingerbread taste like without the ginger?

Some of them wouldn't have much taste at all. That's one thing spices and other seasonings do—make food tastier. They also

130

make medicine taste better. And spices make some perfumes smell good.

We can buy spices almost everywhere now. But long ago spices were so hard to find they were prized as much as gold! People who were lucky enough to have spices often kept these precious seasonings locked in boxes of silver or gold.

In those days, people hadn't learned how to seal food in cans and jars to make it last longer. They had no refrigerators to keep food from spoiling. When they wanted food to keep for a long time, they packed it away in sugar or salt and used spices to make it taste better.

Across deserts and high mountains, camel caravans brought the spices from far places. Sometimes robbers attacked the caravans and tried to steal the spices.

On the ocean, men in tall sailing ships went halfway around the world searching for the islands where spices grow. If pirates didn't capture the ships, and if they weren't sunk in ocean storms, the shipowners traded their gold and jewels for spices.

As if the real dangers weren't
enough, people made up wild
stories about the dangers faced
by spice hunters.

One story told how all the pepper in the world grew on trees
guarded by poisonous snakes.
Before they could get the pepper,
brave men had to kill the snakes
by burning down the trees. After
the fire, all that was left were
black peppers!

But pepper doesn't even grow
on trees. Pepper grows on vines.
The pepper berries, which are
red, are picked just before they
ripen and are then placed in the
sun to dry. As the sun bakes the
berries, they become wrinkled
and turn black. This is how
whole pepper looks at the grocery
store.

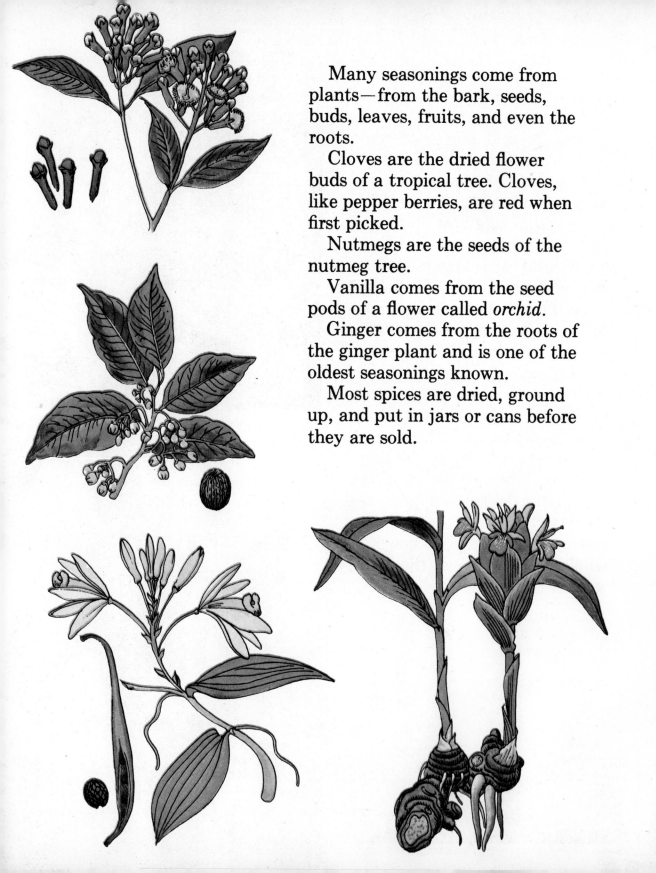

Many seasonings come from plants—from the bark, seeds, buds, leaves, fruits, and even the roots.

Cloves are the dried flower buds of a tropical tree. Cloves, like pepper berries, are red when first picked.

Nutmegs are the seeds of the nutmeg tree.

Vanilla comes from the seed pods of a flower called *orchid*.

Ginger comes from the roots of the ginger plant and is one of the oldest seasonings known.

Most spices are dried, ground up, and put in jars or cans before they are sold.

Here is a rhyme that someone
wrote more than a hundred years
ago about the spice ships and the
wonderful smell of spices:

A Ship Comes In
(Salem — 1830)

From Java, Sumatra, and old Cathay
Another ship is home today.

Now in the heat of the noonday sun
They are unloading cinnamon.

And even here in Town House Square
The spicy fragrance fills the air.

Oh, nothing is quite so exciting to me
As a ship just home from the China Sea.

So I will go down to the harbor soon
And stand around all afternoon.

Kept in Stone

How would you like to see an animal or a plant that lived millions of years ago? You can if you find a fossil. Lots of people find the remains of millions-of-years-old animals and plants in stone. There may be some near where you live.

Plants and animals that are found in stone are called *fossils*.

Many fossils look very much as they did when they were alive.

Some fossils look like careful tracings of a leaf or an animal's backbone. (Enough fossil bones to rebuild a whole dinosaur's skeleton are sometimes found.)

Have you ever pressed a coin into clay and seen the picture that it leaves? Some fossils look as if they've been pressed into clay. The animal really isn't there at all—there's just a kind of picture of it left in the stone.

Fossils are not always easy to find. That's because not all of the animals and plants that were alive millions of years ago have turned to stone or become part of a stone.

This fish *did* become a fossil. It lived in a lake millions of years ago. When it died, it sank to the bottom and became covered with soft, oozy mud. After its flesh had wasted away, its bones were held together by the mud.

As millions of years went by, the lake dried up. Then it was filled with dust and dirt blown by the winds. The bones of the fish stayed where they were.

Later, slowly . . . slowly . . . through the years, the bottom and the sides of the lake—and the dust and dirt that filled it— all turned to stone. But one part of the stone was different—the part where the fish bones were.

The part of the stone that held the fossil of the fish might never have been discovered by some lucky fossil hunter if it weren't for dust-filled winds. These winds scraped the stone that had once been under the lake. They scraped deeper and deeper. (Have you ever sandpapered a stone or a piece of wood? The winds acted the way sandpaper does, only they kept scraping for millions of years.) Finally, the part of the stone that held the fish was uncovered. Dusty winds are among the fossil hunters' best helpers.

Trickling rainwater is another helper. It finds cracks in stone and in cold weather freezes and breaks the stone. Then the fossils are easier to find.

Earthquakes roll big stones around and sometimes uncover fossils.

Road-building machines and scooping machines dig down to rocks where fossils are buried.

Would you like to become a fossil hunter? You won't need a bow and arrow or a net or a lasso. All you need is a pair of sharp eyes.

You can go fossil hunting at the seashore. The tides and waves often wash up fossils from the bottom of the sea. Gravel pits, empty fields, and even vacant lots are good places for fossil hunting. Look for a crumbly, dark-colored rock called *shale*. It often has fossil plants in it.

The sides of hills that roads have cut through and the sides of creeks and dried-up ditches are often happy hunting grounds for fossil hunters.

You can even see fossils downtown in the city. Look for them in the marble walls and steps of banks and libraries and courthouses.

Happy hunting!

When Is a Frog Not a Frog?

Rug-o-jum. Rug-o-jum. This frog's loud "talk" sometimes keeps people awake at night.

When it was very young—about a month old—it looked very different.

When the frog was about one month old, it looked like this. It was called a *tadpole* or a *polliwog*. It didn't look at all like a frog.

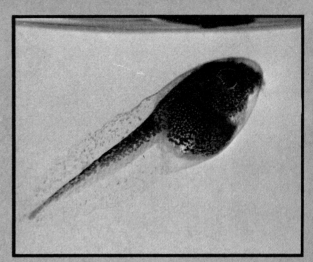

How does the frog change so much in just one year? It all begins when the mother frog lays her eggs in the water.

In a few days, tiny tadpoles wriggle out of the tiny eggs. They have long tails for swimming, and slits, called *gills*, for breathing.

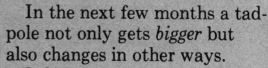
In the next few months a tadpole not only gets *bigger* but also changes in other ways.

It begins to grow a pair of hind legs. Its feet have long toes with webs between them to help it swim. They look like a duck's feet or like the flippers you might wear when you swim.

A little later the tadpole's front legs appear, with small feet that look like little hands.

Its tail is getting shorter and shorter and will soon disappear. It's ready to spend some of its time on land instead of always staying in the water.

It's one year after it was born, and now it's a frog and *looks* like a frog. It has smooth, moist skin and eyes so big that they seem about to pop out of its head. On its long, strong legs, it travels in great leaps.

There's an African frog that can jump *eight feet*. How many feet can you jump?

What is the difference between a frog and a toad?

A toad's skin is dry and bumpy, and because its legs are short, it can only hop, not leap. Most toads live on land, while frogs are able to live and hunt for food both in the water and on land.

Think of Something Big

Sometime, if you want to say something is very big, you might say, "It's as big as a continent."

Not very many things are as big as a continent. Some of the oceans are bigger. And the sun and the moon are bigger. But not many other things that we know much about are bigger.

Continent is the name for a piece of land so big that it's hard to imagine. Look at a globe. Whatever is blue is water. The rest is land, and most of this land is part of a continent.

There are only seven continents on the Earth.

Some of them are surrounded by water, which makes them really big, *big*, BIG islands. But some are attached to each other, such as the continents of Asia and Europe. These two continents together are sometimes called Eurasia.

There are some very big countries in Eurasia—China and the Soviet Union, as well as Spain and France and Italy. Eurasia is so big that it would take a long time to travel by land from Spain at one end to China at the other end. Much of Eurasia is so far north that it is very, very cold. But much of it is far south, where it is very, very hot. The biggest mountains in the world are in Asia. And the greatest number of people live there, too.

The continent closest to Eurasia is Africa. The two continents are attached to each other by the Isthmus of Suez, a narrow piece of land through which a boat canal has been built. Most of the black people of the world come from Africa. In the hot, green jungles and on the grassy plains, there are many wild animals— elephants, lions, giraffes, and crocodiles. There is much mining of diamonds and gold in Africa.

Some of the oldest countries in the world, and many of the newest, are in Africa.

146

Far across the oceans from Eurasia and Africa are two other continents—North America and South America.

Canada, the United States, and Mexico are the three biggest countries in North America. The continent of Asia has the highest mountains, but North America has the biggest hole in the ground —the Grand Canyon. North America starts near the North Pole. Far, far in the south, it gets narrow. Where it joins South America, at the Isthmus of Panama, it is so narrow that it is like the tail of a great animal.

South America, too, gets narrow as it keeps on going south— toward the Antarctic Regions, where it finally ends. There are high mountains all the way down its west coast. Two of the biggest countries in South America are Brazil, with its great, wet jungles, and Argentina, where cowboys, called *gauchos,* ride their horses on big cattle ranches.

The continent of Antarctica is all by itself way down at the South Pole. You wouldn't want to live there. It is a rocky continent covered almost everywhere by thick ice that never melts.

There are tall icy mountains in Antarctica, and it is so cold that nothing grows except a little moss in a few places, and *lichens,* which are something like moss. Oh, yes, the birds that can swim and walk but can't fly—*penguins*—live there.

There is one more continent—Australia. It is the smallest. It lies in the world's biggest ocean, the Pacific. Unusual animals, such as the kangaroo and the koala bear, are found in Australia. The middle of Australia is a hot, rocky desert. Most of the people live around the edges of the continent, near the ocean, where there are great cities and harbors.

Rivers of Jewels

Perhaps it happened this way:

One dark night in a faraway land some sailors came ashore on a sand beach to cook their meal. Their ship was carrying blocks of *soda ash*, which had been dug out of the ground. The soda ash looked a little like hard salt and was used for making soap. The sailors brought ashore a few large blocks of the soda ash in order to make a fireplace for their cooking pot. They made an extra big fire.

As the sailors huddled around the fire, cooking their meal, a strange and wonderful thing began to happen.

"Rivers of jewels!" one of the sailors shouted.

The others looked where he pointed. Shiny, tiny streams were flowing out of the fire like slow-moving snakes. They glittered and sparkled.

When the "rivers of jewels" had cooled, the sailors discovered that these streams had become hard and smooth. They could pick up pieces and see the flickering firelight through them.

The heated sand and soda ash had melted together and become *glass*.

Whether glass was discovered this way or another way no one really knows, but it probably was an accident—no matter how or when it happened.

How could white sand and soda ash turn into glass? Even today we do not know exactly why. But after people learned that glass could be made from sand, they tried to find even better ways to make it. Some men learned how to put a long pipe—somewhat like a giant soda straw—into the hot, gooey glass while it was cooking and lift some out on the end of the pipe. Then they could blow it

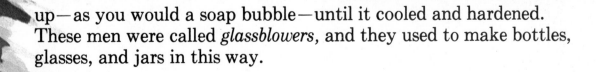

up—as you would a soap bubble—until it cooled and hardened. These men were called *glassblowers*, and they used to make bottles, glasses, and jars in this way.

Later, glassblowers learned to let the bubble of glass go flat while they quickly spun the pipe in their hands until it formed a flat sheet. When the sheet cooled, they broke off the pipe where it was held fast in the hardened glass. This gave them clear glass, which they then cut up into windowpanes.

But people didn't like the looks of the broken-off parts in their windowpanes. They called them *bull's-eyes*. In England, a picture of the king's crown was stamped over the bull's-eyes to hide them. From then on, this kind of glass was known as *crown glass*. (Today, bull's-eyes are considered very valuable by people who collect antiques.)

Soon men learned that by polishing glass with powdered sand and other materials, they could make it even clearer and easier to see through.

Then, by adding other materials to the sand and soda ash and using machines, men discovered ways to make glass in different forms and colors. Glass can be spun like wool or can be very stiff. It can be made so stretchy that it can be bounced upon like a trampoline or it can be twisted like a corkscrew. It can be made almost as strong as iron.

What will glass be like in the future?

Not only windows but also whole houses—which will seem almost magical—may be made of glass. In a glass house, all heat and light will come from the walls, which will turn different shades, depending on how much light there is. On the sunny side of the house, the walls will be dark, like your sunglasses, to cut down the brightness. On the shady side of the house, the glass will be completely clear to let all the light in. But from outside the house, people will not be able to see in at all!

There seems to be no end to the things that can be done with glass.

The Gloomy Gorilla

The largest of the manlike apes
   would rather be alone,
And so he keeps his family where
   the jungle's overgrown.
There he is on that *hill, a gorilla!*

This ape eats fruit and vegetables.
   He doesn't kill for food,
Although he looks quite angry, and
   he has a gloomy mood.
His glare gives you a *chill—a gorilla.*

Although he sometimes swings from trees,
   most often he is found
With mate and young ones, finding food
   below, down on the ground.
It takes a lot to *fill—a gorilla.*

Sometimes he stands up like a man
   and walks as man does, too.
I'd never think he was one, though,
   and shake his hand. Would you?
No matter how he walks, he's *still a gorilla.*

He's very strong, his arms are long,
   and when he must, he can
Defend his home from other beasts.
   His only fear is man!
It's not easy for beasts to *kill a gorilla.*

153

Although gorillas look ferocious, they are really rather quiet apes. They live in family groups in the thickest parts of the jungles.

A gorilla's feet, hands, and wrinkled face are bare and black. His fur may be short or long, depending on where he lives.

The short-haired gorilla lives in the hot, damp, tropical forests of western Africa.

The long-haired gorilla lives in the cooler air in the high mountains of central Africa.

A gorilla's arms are so long they almost touch the ground, even when he is standing up!

Some wild mountain gorillas weigh as much as you, your father, and your mother all weigh together.

At night the father gorilla sleeps on the ground. But the mother and the baby gorillas sleep in big nests of sticks and leaves on the ground, or in the lower branches of trees, where they are safer from prowling animals.

High-Flying Helper

High, higher, higher still! Fast, faster, faster still! That's the hawk! Some hawks fly so high that you need binoculars to see them. Some fly so fast that they can pass a small airplane.

A hawk soaring and swooping high in the air is not just having fun—it's hunting. When it spots a meal, it folds its wings in close to its sides and dives down. Some hawks can dive at a speed of more than 300 miles an hour.

A hawk looks mean because it has big, round eyes, long, sharp claws, and a strong, curved beak. But a hawk needs to have these things because it eats only meat of animals it catches alive. The things about it that look mean and cruel to us are what make it a good hunter.

Because it hunts mice and rats—which eat farm crops—the hawk is a good friend to the farmer. Unfortunately, many people who do not know that this bird is a friend shoot it. So laws have been passed to protect it.

Even most of the little hawks—which fly low—are helpful. They eat grasshoppers and other insects that eat the plants that grow in gardens and on farms.

High-flying hawks have their nests in high places. Some nest on cliffs. A few even nest on the ledges of tall city buildings. The marsh hawk, a low-flying bird, nests on the ground.

Big or little, all hawks are beautiful flyers—fun to watch—and most of them are good friends to us.

The Wonderful Whirlybird

This helicopter is about to land on the top of a tall office building right in the middle of a big city.

It is dropping straight down. Just before you think it is going to crash, it will slow down and come gently to rest. It will wait until people get out to go to their offices and then fly straight up and away over the tops of the buildings.

This helicopter isn't going to land. Like a hummingbird hovering over a flower, it's standing still in the air while a rope ladder is lowered to rescue a man and a boy from a mountain cliff. When they're safely inside, the pilot will fly them home—zigging and zagging, flying backward and forward, even sideways, between the dangerous mountains.

Standing still in the air and going straight up and straight down are some of the things helicopters can do that other aircraft can't.

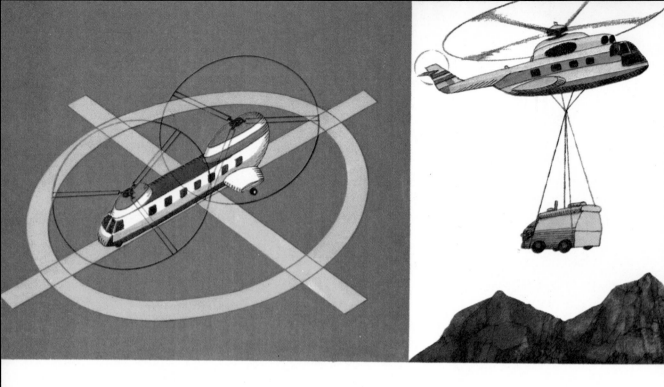

Most airplanes need long runways for taking off and for landing. Airports have to be built far away from the middle of cities because there isn't enough room between the buildings for airplanes to land.

But a helicopter has a special, enormous propeller, or *rotor*, that whirls around on top of it. This lets the helicopter take off or land in a space not much bigger than the helicopter itself.

Airplanes have to fly very fast to stay in the air. If they didn't fly fast, they would fall. But the pilot of a helicopter, or a whirly-bird, as it is called sometimes, can fly as slowly as he wishes to.

Helicopters can lift heavy steel beams to the top of a building.

They can get in between trees and houses to spray farmers' grain and vegetables so that these crops will be safe from insects that might eat them.

They fly into narrow places between high cliffs to help fire fighters put out forest fires.

Some hospitals have whirlybird landing pads on their roofs so that people who are sick or hurt can be brought there in a hurry.

We keep finding new jobs for the wonderful whirlybirds.

They Sound Like Spinning Tops

It's like a humming jewel in the air.

Its wings fan so fast that you can't see them move. It flies forward or straight up or straight down. It can even fly backward! Its wings are a flashing blur in the sunlight and make a sound like the soft hum of a spinning top.

That's probably how the hummingbird got its name. Somebody a long time ago heard this soft hum and gave the bird its name. A hummingbird is less afraid of people than most birds are. It doesn't always fly away when you come close.

Look for a hummingbird in a flower garden. It's so pretty that it's almost like a flower that has left its stem and is hovering in the air. It can stay almost still in the air while it dips its long, sharp beak deep inside a flower. Its thin, curled-over tongue sucks up the sweet flower juices—like the straw you use for sucking up a tasty drink from a glass.

Hummingbirds are among the smallest birds alive. They're not much bigger than bumblebees. They're so tiny that their nests are the size of a doll's teacup. And their eggs look like tiny white beans.

You almost never see these bright-colored little birds on the ground. Their legs are too weak and too small for hopping. But they do have strong feet for holding on to leafy branches. So that's the best place to see a hummingbird nest—in leafy tree branches. The nest is made to look like a small bump on the branch—good for hiding the hummingbird from enemies and for protecting its babies.

The Jewels That Mountains Wear

How much ice did you ever see in one place? An ice tray full? A skating rink full? A pond full? A river frozen from bank to bank? That's a lot of ice. But there are places in the world where there is more. Much more.

You know how high mountains are. There are places where the space between mountains is crammed and jammed and packed full of ice.

This kind of ice is called a *glacier*.

Glaciers are the jewels that mountains wear. Sometimes they are as blue as sapphires. When the sun shines on them, glaciers may look like gold. At sunset they may look sparkling ruby red. By starlight they're all diamonds and silver.

How did all this ice, this glacier, get up there so high in the mountains?

First, snow fell on the mountains.

High up, where it is always very cold, some of the snow never melts, not even in summer. More snow kept falling on the snow that was already there. Year after year the snow grew deeper.

It grew so deep and heavy that the snow at the bottom was crushed by the weight of the snow at the top. It was crushed so much that it was packed into ice. (Have you ever packed a snowball between your hands? You do this by squeezing the snow until it becomes almost like ice instead of soft, loose snow.)

There was another thing that helped make the ice. In the summers some of the snow on top was melted by the sun. The melted snow water sank down, mixing with the bottom snow and freezing it.

This packing and pressing and freezing kept on until the whole mountain valley was solid ice—a glacier.

And then . . .
The glacier started moving!

That's another surprising thing about a glacier. It moves. You might say that a glacier is a river of ice moving between the mountains. It doesn't move as fast as a river. It moves so slowly you can't even see it move. Usually it moves no more than a few feet a day. But it keeps moving, and finally it gets somewhere.

It scrapes the sides of the mountains as it moves and tears off chunks of rocks as big as a house. Big rocks, little rocks, sand, and clay—they're all scooped up by the moving ice and carried along.

As the glacier moves down the mountain into warmer weather, the ice begins to melt. The icy water rushes into streams, and the rocks and sand are dropped wherever the glacier melts.

But sometimes a glacier moves down a mountain that is next to the ocean. When this happens, huge chunks of the glacier break off and go plunging into the water. And the glacier, which was once a river of ice, becomes many floating islands of ice.

These giant floating pieces of the glacier are called *icebergs*.

168

The Biggest Ice Cube

If you ever see a big, BIG chunk of ice floating in the ocean, it's an iceberg. Icebergs start on land and slide off into the ocean. What a *splash!* Because—think about it—even little icebergs are as big as a school bus. Big ones are longer than a freight train and as high as a skyscraper.

Icebergs start in the part of the world where it's always cold—far away near the North and South poles.

Something you'd probably never guess about an iceberg is that the big chunk of ice that floats above the water is only a small part of the whole iceberg. Most of this floating giant is underwater and doesn't show.

This picture shows you the rest of the iceberg, the large part that is hidden beneath the cold, dark water.

If you would like to see the way an iceberg floats, here's an easy experiment you can do at home.

Fill a glass half full of very cold water.

Drop an ice cube into the glass of water.

Looking through the outside of the glass, see how much of the ice is above the water and how much of it is below.

Your piece of ice floats exactly the way an iceberg floats.

169

Icebergs look like islands of ice. But when you think about it, icebergs really are not like islands. Islands go all the way down to the bottom of the ocean. They must stay where they are—they can't float or move. But icebergs float and move.

Icebergs also melt and disappear. They melt when they float away from freezing waters to warmer waters under a hot sun.

Some icebergs look like giant wedding cakes, while others look like shining white castles. When they catch the red and gold colors of the sunset, they all look like giant flames.

But these same beautiful icebergs are very dangerous when they float, big and silent, into the path of a ship. Many ships used to be wrecked because they hit an iceberg floating in the ocean. Today this hardly ever happens.

Now there is a special fleet of small ships, called the International
Ice Patrol. These small ships do nothing but look for icebergs that
other ships might run into. When one of the patrol ships
sights an iceberg, it radios a warning to all the ships in nearby
waters. Sometimes iceberg patrol sailors break up an especially
dangerous iceberg with explosives. That makes many big splashes
and keeps the ocean safer for ships, because the broken-up iceberg
melts faster.

But next spring more icebergs float down from the Far North,
and so the iceberg patrol keeps watching.

Friends or Enemies?

Swat them! Spray them! Or shoo them away! These are the things most people do when they see

ants crawling near the
    picnic baskets,
bees buzzing around
    their heads,
a spider hanging from
    its web,
flies settling on food,
or when they hear mosquitoes humming.

Anything to get rid of these pests!

When insects or other bugs annoy us at a picnic—or anywhere else—we think of them as pests. But if you were a fly trying to get away from a swatter-swinging person, you might find the person a bit of a pest!

Actually, most insects are interesting to watch and some are helpful to people.

There are so many different kinds of insects that it would be hard to learn about *all* of them.

Some, such as the beautiful butterflies, have bright colors, shapes, and markings. Others, such as the long, thin praying mantis and the walkingstick, look rather funny.

Insects start out as eggs. When the eggs are hatched, the insect *larvas* are born.

As a larva grows, it grows out of its skin again and again. *Pop!* and a new larva wriggles out to grow some more.

173

A larva may be a very small copy of what it'll look like as a grown-up insect. Or it may be a tiny thing that looks like a worm.

If you like to watch colorful birds swooping overhead or listen to their cheerful singing, you'd better hope that all bugs don't disappear. Many birds need insects to eat—even when they're still babies. Larks, orioles, meadowlarks, finches, sparrows, swallows, warblers, wrens, mockingbirds, chickadees, thrushes, robins, bluebirds, and others would disappear if insects disappeared.

174

Some insects eat the farmers' plants. Moths eat cloth, and termites eat wood. These insects don't know that they are destroying something you need or want. They are only trying to stay alive. But that doesn't help if the thing they are eating happens to be your favorite sweater or your house!

The next time you are annoyed by the insects that visit your picnic, you'll shoo them away. But if you remember all the good things insects do, you may be shooing away a *friend* who is being a pest—not an enemy.

Insects Tune In

If you were an insect, which pair of antennas do you think you would like?

Some antennas are long, and some are short.

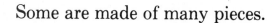

Some antennas have knobs at the ends, and some have hooks.

Some are made of many pieces.

Some look like tiny feathers. Some are used for smelling, and some are used for tasting. Some can feel, and some can hear. Some can do more than one of these things. And not only insects have antennas. Some land and water animals, such as centipedes and lobsters, have them, too.

176

Some insects use their antennas to tell about things that are far away.

A few bushy moths can smell so well with their antennas that they can smell a moth that is more than a mile away and can fly to it—even in the dark of night.

When an ant has found food, it hurries back to the nest. It runs around waving its antennas and touching other ants to signal that food is nearby.

Ants also use their antennas to smell. After finding food, one kind of ant leaves a trail of tiny droplets on its way back to the nest. The other ants smell these droplets and follow the trail to the food.

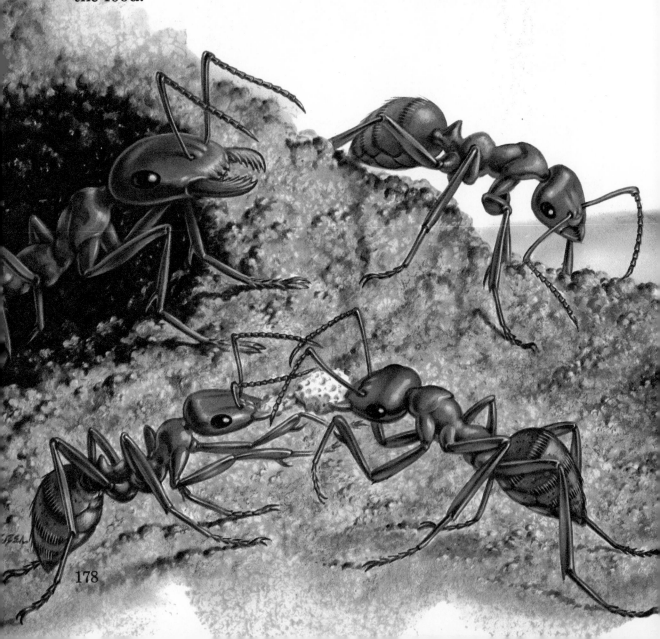

To keep its antennas working well, the ant combs them with round combs that grow on its front legs. Then it cleans the combs with its mouth.

It seems strange to us that antennas can be used to smell, taste, or hear. But if insects could think about how we do these same things, they might look at our noses, tongues, and ears and think, "What funny-looking antennas."

Surrounded by Water

The outside of the Earth is made of land and water. Some very large parts are land, and some very large parts are water.

The very large land parts are *continents.* The very large water parts are *oceans* and *seas.*

On the continents are some smaller water parts—*lakes* and *rivers.* In the oceans and seas are some smaller land parts that are surrounded by water—*islands.* And what you might find on one of the islands is a lake with an island in it!

Islands come in all sizes and shapes.

On a very small island you could walk along the shore and in a little while you'd be back where you started.

The very smallest islands are too small to hold even a house. The largest islands have cities and countries on them.

If you lived in England or Greenland or Japan you would be living on an island. But if you lived on islands as big as these islands, it wouldn't seem as if you were living on an island. You could walk all day and never come to water.

How did the islands ever get there in the first place?

The Earth is always changing—very slowly. Oceans and streams are washing some of the land into the water. The wind blows loose soil away. The Earth's hot insides are pushing land up in some places, while the ground sinks in other places.

Long, long ago, some islands were fiery volcanoes that filled the air with smoke and cinders. Hot rock kept pouring out of them, making the island bigger and bigger. Later, the hot rock cooled, and the islands slowly became the way they are today.

Other islands were once a part of the world's bigger pieces of land, the *continents*. Some of the land was worn away by wind or rain. Some of the land sank. The water from the ocean came in to fill the low places and made a new island.

A row of islands may once have been the tops of mountains in a line of mountains called a *mountain range*.

The Aleutian Islands were probably once a part of a solid mountain range that connected Alaska with the continent called Asia.

The largest island in the world is Greenland, near the cold North Pole. Another big island is Madagascar, where it is hot and rainy. The island of New Zealand has beautiful mountains.

Many of the world's big islands have cities on them. But it is the little islands that are especially fun to live on. On some little islands in the South Seas you can fish in the sunshine and pick coconuts and delicious fruits from the trees.

The Bear That Isn't a Bear

This roly-poly little animal has shiny black eyes that look like wet licorice candy. Its nose is shiny black, too, and is pressed against its face between its bushy gray ears. If you found it under a Christmas tree, you might think it was a toy teddy bear.

But "roly-poly" is a real animal. It lives only in Australia. It is called a *koala*, and it looks so much like a toy bear that you want to turn it around just to see if it has a key in its back so that you can wind it up.

But koalas aren't bears. They belong to the same family as kangaroos. Animals of this family are called *pouch* animals. That's because the mother carries her baby around in a pouch in the front of her stomach. It's like a built-in papoose basket, only it's in the front instead of the back.

When they are first born, koala babies are smaller even than a little finger. Only one koala baby is born at a time. After about six months the koala baby is ready to explore the world. But not on its own feet. It comes out of the pouch and climbs up on its mother's back. For six months it rides on her back everywhere she goes until it's almost as big as she is.

It sounds as if its mother spoils it. But she can be strict when it doesn't behave. If it's too naughty, she'll even put it over her knee and spank it!

The koala drinks dew and eats nothing but leaves from eucalyptus and blue gum trees.

Koalas love people and make wonderful pets. When a koala likes you, it puts its arms around your neck and hugs you!

185

Would You Believe?

Guess how many different living things there are in the world—how many kinds of animals and how many kinds of plants.

Altogether, there are millions of different kinds of living things: From the biggest animal of all—the whale—to animals so tiny you can't see them without a microscope. From the biggest tree in the world—the sequoia—to plants so tiny you can't see them either without a microscope.

Among these millions of different living things, there are some so strange that most people have never even heard about them. Sometimes you might see one in a zoo, but usually to see one you would have to go to the bottom of the ocean, the high places in mountains, under the ground, or far into forests, jungles, deserts, or plains.

You know what a fish looks like. Are you sure? Did you ever see any like the ones on these pages? They live far down in the ocean, where it is always dark. So, some of them make their own light—something like the kind that fireflies make.

You have probably heard about flying fish or swordfish or sawfish. But did you ever hear about a fish that comes out of the water and goes about on the land? The mudskipper does this. It can stay out of the water for a very long time. Its face looks a little like a frog's, and out of the water it uses its front fins like hands. It breathes through its skin. If you happened to be in the right place in Africa, you might see a mudskipper. It hops along so quickly that a man can't catch it.

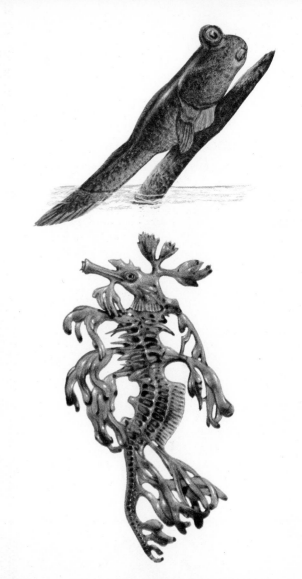

Would you believe that this is a fish? It's called a *sea dragon*, and it lives in the ocean near Australia.

How would you like one of these for a pet? It's a star-nosed mole. It lives in Canada and the United States, in swampy places or near muddy creeks. With its strong claws, it digs long burrows under the ground. It's a good swimmer, too. The 22 pink "fingers" at the top of its head are feelers.

Charles E. Mohr from National Audubon Society

188

Everybody knows what a deer looks like. They're as big as a pony or a horse. Are you sure?

The musk deer is a cunning little creature no bigger than a small dog. It lives among rocky cliffs in the high mountains of Asia.

Paul Popper Limited

But you surely know what a tree looks like. Are you very, very sure?

The bottle tree looks a little like an upside-down tree with its roots in the air instead of in the ground. It holds a lot of water inside its trunk. Sometimes people hollow out old trees and use them for houses.

Howard Uible

Can you tell which are the rocks and which are the plants? It's very hard to tell until the plants bloom!

189

The Ones That Roar

This lion can run faster than your parents are allowed to drive a car through town. It weighs as much as two heavy men.

When angry or hungry, a lion will charge with great speed. But the rest of the time its steps are slow and lazy.

Lions like company. They live in groups in grasslands, desert places, and rocky hills. During the day they rest in the shade. Some lions even climb trees and rest in the branches.

Both the mother and father lions hunt for food, usually at night. Like other cats, they can see well in dim light. They hunt grazing animals, such as wildebeests, zebras, and gazelles. Unless they are very hungry, most lions will not attack man or a large animal, such as a giraffe or a hippopotamus. Lions that live near a village may steal donkeys or goats or even small cows. Imagine teeth and necks strong enough to lift a cow over a fence!

Lions hunting in groups have been known to work together to catch a fast-running gazelle. First, some of the lions hide. The others chase the gazelle toward them, and the hiding lions spring out and catch it. When a lion hunts alone, it sneaks up on an animal and leaps on it swiftly.

Except for African animal parks, there are not many places left where lions still run free. But you can see them at a circus or a zoo. You would know the father lion by that big fur collar—his *mane*—and by his sandy-colored coat and the dark tuft on his tail.

The mother lion is the same color and a little smaller and has no mane. When her cubs are born, they are no bigger than loaves of bread. And they have dark spots, which disappear later.

You may think of lions as roaring, but they growl, grunt, and cough, too. Sometimes they even purr like giant pussycats.

Monsters That Live Today

Is this a dinosaur?

No, it's not a dinosaur. It's a lizard that's alive today. It's called a *land iguana,* and it lives on a sunny island. It is no longer than a big dog, and although it looks fierce, it won't hurt you.

Not all lizards are the kind that scare you to look at them. A little lizard called the *American chameleon* is pretty and graceful and friendly. These tiny creatures help us by scampering around and eating harmful insects, which they catch with their long, sticky tongues. They can't really change color when they want to, but their skins do change from brown to green when there are changes in light and temperature.

There are many kinds of lizards. They may be almost any color —green, gray, red, brown, blue, yellow, or black. Some have stripes, and some have spots. Some are longer than a man, and some are so tiny you could hold them between your fingers.

Most lizards have dry, scaly skin; strong, short legs; long toes; and sharp claws. Some have bumps on their heads, and sharp, bony collars around their necks.

Some lizards have spiny scales under their toes, which help them cling to rocks, leaves, or branches. They can climb around in trees so quickly that you can hardly see them move. Some can whisk up a wall so smooth that you wonder how they can possibly stay on.

Other lizards can stand up and run on their back legs.

Some lizards have no legs at all. They move like snakes. One is called a *glass lizard* because it can break into several pieces if its tail is pulled.

197

There is one lizard—the *draco*—that is called the *flying dragon*. It can't fly the way a bird does, but it has a tough skin, which it can spread out to make wings. It can jump from a tree and sail a long way through the air.

Although there are no dragons except in stories, the *marine* or *water iguana* is a lizard that *looks* like a dragon. A strong swimmer, it makes its home near the ocean and eats seaweed.

There are other lizards that protect themselves in the curious manner of the glass lizard. If another animal attacks and grabs one of these lizards by the tail, the lizard leaves its tail behind and scurries away to safety—and to grow a new tail!

The *gila monster* is one of the few lizards that are dangerous. The gila lives in the desert. It is black and pink or orange, which makes it easy to see. That's a good thing because the gila bites and hangs on, and its bite is poisonous.

The Hard-Shelled Lobster

A lobster has
Feelers for feeling, eyes on stalks,
Paddles for swimming, legs for walks.
A tail that steers, a shell for wearing,
A claw for crunching, a claw for tearing.

Lobsters have many parts—so many parts sticking out of their bodies that you'd think they would get all tangled up. But they don't!

Every part does a job that helps keep these hard-shelled creatures alive.

Tiny fringed paddles called *swimmerets* cover a lobster's stomach and help it swim. But when a lobster wants to go somewhere in a hurry, it uses its fan-shaped tail. With just one flip, its tail moves a lobster so far and so fast that it seems as if a blur is sweeping along. But look at the direction the lobster is going. *Backward!* (No, lobsters don't bump into things as we would. Their eyes are attached to stalks that move, so they can see in almost every direction!)

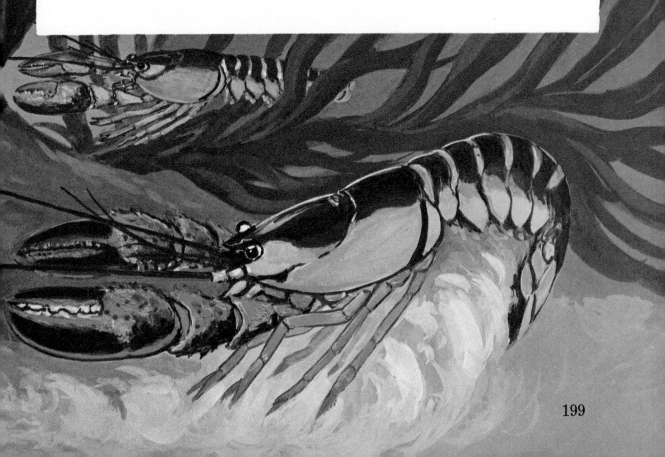

Lobsters swim forward and sideways, too, but not as fast as backward. During the day they hardly move at all. Instead, they stay hidden under a tangle of seaweed or dig burrows in the dark, muddy ocean bottom.

Night is their hunting time, when they poke into rocky corners of the sea floor, looking for shellfish, snails, sea urchins, and starfish, alive or dead. Their feelers, called *antennas*, help them find food and warn them when dangerous enemies—big fish and seals—are nearby.

Lobsters have lots of legs. Four of their eight walking legs have tiny pincerlike claws. In front of the walking legs a lobster waves two great claws. One of these claws is heavy enough to dig through gravel and sand for buried shellfish and strong enough to crush the shells. The other has sharp sawlike teeth for grabbing and cutting food.

Without the hard, tough shells that cover them, lobsters wouldn't be safe from their enemies very long. And if there weren't joints—hinges—dividing their shells into sections, lobsters couldn't move at all.

But while their bodies grow, their shells stay the same size. So whenever a growing lobster becomes too tight in its shell, it just climbs right out of it! This happens many times during the first year of a lobster's life and once a year afterward. It is always a time of danger for a lobster. It takes a few weeks for a new shell to harden, and during this time a lobster stays hidden in deep rocky holes or in thick seaweed that grows on the ocean bottom.

Lobster babies hatch from eggs laid in deep water. They are born without swimmerets, so they paddle with their hairy little legs, snapping up any food they can find floating on top of the water. After a few weeks they sink to the bottom of the sea and live down there for the rest of their lives.

The Iron Horse

Whoo-whoo-whoo-oo-oo-oo-o-o-o . . .

The whistle's blowing. Clear the track. Here comes the locomotive.

And here comes the horse!

They're running a race. Does that seem silly? Anyone knows a railroad locomotive can beat a horse in a race.

But that wasn't always true. About 200 years ago, when locomotives had just been invented, a locomotive called *Tom Thumb* ran a race with a horse. And the horse won!

A little while before this, horses instead of locomotives were used for pulling trains. The trains they pulled were called *horsecars*.

202

Wagons that had steam engines and pulled other wagons on tracks were called *iron horses*. Today there are thousands and thousands of "iron horses" pulling trains on railroad tracks all over the world. But they are no longer called *iron horses*. Instead, they are called *locomotives*—steam, diesel, and electric.

The first locomotive that really worked was built by Richard Trevithick, an Englishman. He named it the *Catch Me Who Can*. (It didn't go so fast. Almost anybody could have caught it!)

The first locomotive to carry people was called *Locomotion No. 1*. The freight cars were filled with coal and sacks of flour. The passengers sat on top of the coal and the flour!

The *Stourbridge Lion* was built in England and sent across the ocean in a boat. It was the first locomotive to run in the United States.

Some locomotives once used bonfires as headlights!
Bang!
Old-time locomotive boilers sometimes exploded. Bales of cotton behind the engine protected the passengers. And a band drowned out the locomotive's frightening noise!

Some old-time locomotives were as beautiful as circus wagons.

Before there were many fences, cows and other farm animals often wandered onto railroad tracks. "Cowcatchers" on the front of locomotives could push them to one side without running over them.

Steam locomotives are still used in some parts of the world. This is one of the giants.

The kind now most used in the United States is a diesel locomotive.

A diesel locomotive is a combination automobile and electric power station! It has an engine like an automobile's. But the engine doesn't make the locomotive go. It runs a *generator,* a machine that makes electricity. The electricity runs electric motors right on the locomotive's wheels.

An electric locomotive draws its electricity from wires overhead. It may also get electricity from a third rail beneath the train.

Switch engines are big diesels that switch freight and passenger cars from one train to another. These squat, powerful locomotives are the workhorses of the railroad yards.

A Switchmobile is both switch engine and highway truck! It can climb across tracks, run on them, weave through city traffic, or even cross open country without any road at all.

This locomotive has jet engines! It can flash along the rails at *170* miles an hour. That's a lot faster than the little *Tom Thumb* that the horse beat!

Locomotives of the future will run themselves! Scientists are already experimenting with a train that has just a computer in some central station for an engineer!

Where Does Medicine Come From?

In the green jungle a jaguar crouched on a tree limb. Through a tangle of leaves and vines it watched two hunters. When the hunters came close, the jaguar got ready to spring.

The man with the gun looked up and saw the jaguar—too late. There was no time to lift his gun and shoot.

But—amazingly—the jaguar didn't come clawing and biting at him through the air. The fierce animal just fell off the tree limb and lay helpless on the ground. . . .

What made the jaguar fall?

The hunters' guide had brought the beast down with a blowgun. He had put the blowgun to his lips and blown a dart at the jaguar.

But how could a little dart stop such a big, fierce animal?

The tip of the dart had been dipped in a poison—called *curare*—made from certain trees in the jungle. Curare poison *paralyzes*, or deadens, the muscles in the body so that they do not work.

When scientists heard about this remarkable poison that was used in the Amazon jungle in South America, they got some and experimented with it. They discovered that when used in big doses, curare will kill. But when it's used in very tiny doses, it is a good medicine. It can be used to relax the muscles of people during operations, which helps the surgeon do a good job.

How would you like to take medicine made from these things: a pinch of gold dust, a spoonful of ashes of a dried lizard, 20 powdered beetles, some burned cat's hair, and two mashed onions?

Many years ago if you had a stomachache, the doctor might have given you a medicine containing such things. The worse the medicine tasted, the better it was supposed to be for you!

Not all the old recipes for medicine were as bad as this one. Usually medicines were made from ground-up bark and leaves, berries and seeds, roots and flowers.

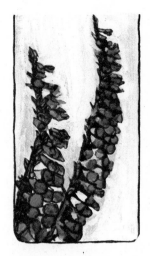

Some of our medicines still come from plants, all kinds of plants —even weeds. The leaves of *foxglove*, a garden flower, contain something that is used to help people who have heart disease. The leaves and roots of a poisonous weed called *deadly nightshade* produce a medicine used by the eye doctor.

Castor oil is made from the beans of the castor-oil plant. Pods of the opium poppy are used to make drugs that stop pain.

Many of these medicines are now made from chemicals instead of being taken from growing plants. But some of today's factory-made medicines are just copies of the natural medicines that were used long ago by the Chinese, the Africans, the American Indians, and others.

Not so very many years ago a very important medicine was discovered in a very unexpected place—moldy bread. This medicine, *penicillin,* and others like it are called *antibiotics*. They help fight many different diseases. They are sometimes in the "shots" the doctor gives you to help you get well quickly.

A Mouse in the House

Do you like to eat cereal? Or nuts? Or apples? Or tasty sandwiches made with bacon or cheese or peanut butter?

House mice do, too! In fact, they enjoy nearly all the foods that people like to eat. And since they also need a warm place in which to live and sleep, your house would suit them just fine!

They don't ask anybody. They don't pay rent. They just move in. You hardly ever see them come or go. You just know they're there when you hear them scampering through the wall or along the floor . . . or gnawing a hole in the wall or the cupboard door . . . or when you see their teeth marks on food you left out in the kitchen.

Wherever there are houses in the world, there are likely to be house mice. They sleep in the daytime, curled up in their warm cozy nests behind the walls or under the floor.

It's quite safe in the house for a house mouse . . . unless you set a trap for it or have a house cat— a house mouse's worst enemy!

Not all mice live in houses. Many live in fields. Field mice have many enemies—foxes, weasels, and big birds, especially owls that hunt for food at night. That's the time when field mice, as well as other mice, are busiest.

Field mice usually build their nests under the roots of big trees or under thick bushes—where they feel safe and where there are other plants to eat.

But, like house mice, furry field mice often turn out to be pests because they also eat many of the foods that people eat. Field mice eat corn, wheat, rice, and almost every other crop that farmers plant in their fields.

In the winter, field mice often move into a nearby house. Then they eat all the things house mice eat. The only way you can tell them from house mice is by their larger size.

J. M. Conrader

Mother mice have lots of babies—tiny pink babies that keep their eyes shut for a long time.

All mice have long, sharp teeth for chewing. Most mice have small ears, so close to their heads that it's hard to see them unless you get very near.

Some people think that mice are really small rats. But they are *not*. Although mice are often pests, they aren't nearly so dangerous as rats. Mice don't bite people, but rats sometimes do.

Mice have softer, shorter fur than rats. Their tails are shorter and furry. As long as they aren't gnawing holes in your house or eating your food, mice are nice!

Helen Cruickshank from National Audubon Society

In barns, holes in the wall, attics, cellars—wherever you look you might find mice living there. They also live on ships, under logs, and in tall grass.

If one mouse is a mouse
And one house is a house,
Why does one mouse plus one mouse
   equal two *mice?*
But one house plus one house
   doesn't equal two *hice?*

What's Under the Earth?

Watch out! Step back! A power shovel can pick you up as easily as you can pick up a leaf. This giant shovel can pick up 100 tons of iron rock, or *ore,* in one bite. That's a whole railroad car full of iron ore.

We use iron to build ships and trains and bridges and tall skyscrapers and many other things. We get most of our iron—and a lot of copper and coal—from *strip mines.* These are mines that are close to the top of the earth. Giant power shovels dig down and bite the ore out. They can take one of these big bites every minute. Watch out! Step back! Here it comes again!

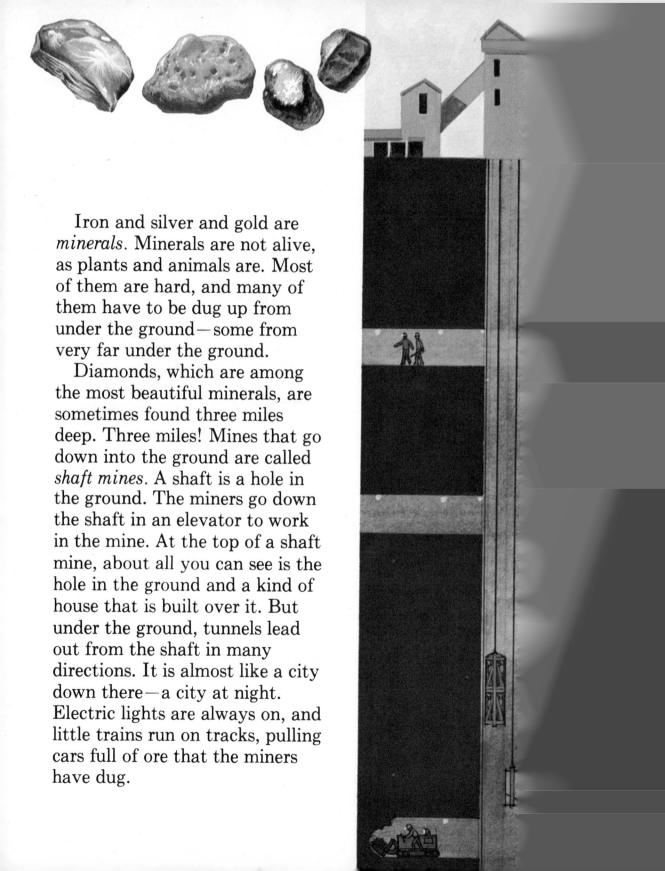

Iron and silver and gold are *minerals*. Minerals are not alive, as plants and animals are. Most of them are hard, and many of them have to be dug up from under the ground—some from very far under the ground.

Diamonds, which are among the most beautiful minerals, are sometimes found three miles deep. Three miles! Mines that go down into the ground are called *shaft mines*. A shaft is a hole in the ground. The miners go down the shaft in an elevator to work in the mine. At the top of a shaft mine, about all you can see is the hole in the ground and a kind of house that is built over it. But under the ground, tunnels lead out from the shaft in many directions. It is almost like a city down there—a city at night. Electric lights are always on, and little trains run on tracks, pulling cars full of ore that the miners have dug.

Not all mines go straight down from the top of the ground. When minerals are taken from a hill or a mountain, tunnels usually go in from the side. Tunnel mines are called *drift mines*. Small railroad cars take the miners in and haul the minerals out.

Instead of a shovel, this miner is using a strong jet of water to dig out the mineral called *gold*. Gold is sometimes found loosely mixed with gravel. The miner turns on a powerful hose and washes the gold and gravel out of the hill. The gold and gravel then go through long boxes, or *sluices,* that are open at both ends. Water washes the gravel through the sluices. But the gold, which is heavier, separates from the gravel and sinks to the bottom.

218

Long, long ago there was a time when nobody wanted to be a miner. The men who worked in the mines were captured slaves or prisoners of war. Falling rocks, poisonous air, flooding water, and blinding darkness made the ancient mines about as dangerous as a battlefield.

Most mines today are safer. And the work is not so hard.

Machines do most of the drilling and digging. Elevators and escalators do the heavy lifting.

Safety inspectors visit each mine regularly.

Engineers are always at work to make better machines to do the job faster.

Because scientists find places where minerals are most likely to be, miners don't have to dig so much. The mines can be smaller and less rambling, and they are less likely to cave in.

These buildings are above an abandoned mine. Nobody is working in the mine. Nobody will ever work there again. All the minerals are gone. They are gone for good.

Minerals are not like plants. They do not grow every spring from seeds that are planted in the ground. It takes millions of years for minerals to form.

We don't know whether we'll ever use up all the minerals that are in the earth. But just in case we do, scientists are working to make things to take the place of minerals.

Funny Money

Long ago, people in one part of the world didn't go to an office or a factory to earn money. They found their money on the ground. The money was large, round, and flat. It looked just like what it was—a stone!

Because they were special stones and very hard to find, they were valuable.

The larger the stone, the more valuable it was. The smallest money stones—about the size of a dinner plate—might buy a fish, a baby pig, or some vegetables.

Slaves carried the heavier stones for the men and women who went shopping.

The richest men had stones too big and heavy to carry around. These men left their stones in front of their houses so that everyone could see how rich they were.

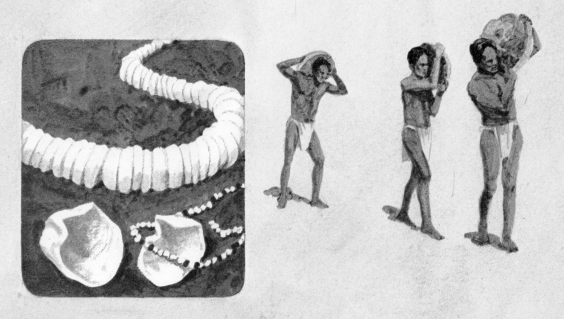

People in some places found their money along the seashore—red, black, and white shells.

The women broke the shells into little pieces, polished them, made small holes in them, and strung them on strings.

One string of shell money would buy food. A hundred strings might buy a canoe or a cow.

Some people could eat their money! They made money out of salt, which they shaped into little bricks. The bricks were all of the same size and value. They were stamped with a picture of the king to show that the king would accept the salt as money. If the king would accept it, then everyone else would, too.

Salt money wasn't heavy or awkward like stone money or so hard to find as shell money. But when it rained, the money might melt!

Finally, people started using metal for money—copper and silver and gold. Metal wasn't easily damaged by water or heat or time. And since there wasn't very much of it, everyone wanted it.

Metal money was made in many shapes—in chunks, disks, or rings. Some of it was shaped and stamped like salt money.

Metal money was certainly better than salt or shell or stone money. But if you have very much of it, metal money is hard to carry around. It is heavy and takes up a lot of space. So today we also have paper money, with numbers printed on it to show how much the money is worth.

225

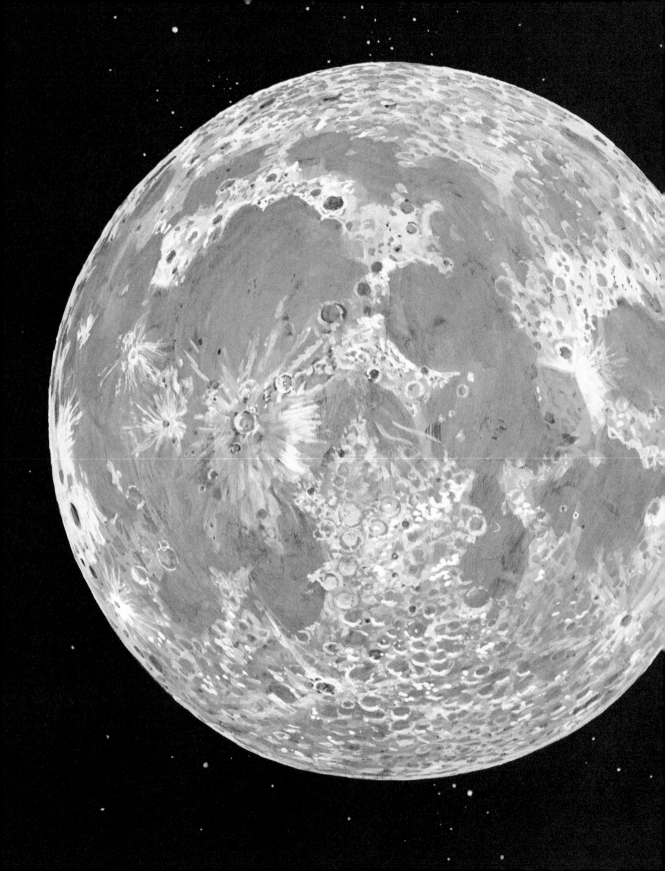

Meet the Man in the Moon

Did you ever look up at the moon and think you saw a man's face there?

When the moon is round and full, the shadows of the moon mountains and the lines of the moon valleys sometimes seem to show a giant nose and mouth and eyes. At least, some people think so.

If there were a man on the moon—instead of mountains and valleys that just look like the face of a man—what would he be like?

He would not be like anyone you know. He would not be like anyone *anybody* knows.

If the man on the moon were bothered by too much heat or cold the way Earth people are, he could not stay on the moon.

The moon becomes very, very hot. It becomes as hot as boiling water. And the moon becomes very, very cold. It becomes colder than ice.

Whatever part of the moon the sun shines on is hot and bright. The rest of the moon is cold and dark.

Look at the moon every night. Draw a picture of it. You will see that it changes every night until finally it has changed back to the way it looked the first time you drew it. Count your pictures. It will take 29 nights for the moon to change and then change back again.

227

If the man on the moon had to breathe to stay alive, he couldn't live on the moon because there's no air there. (He'd have to carry an oxygen tank, as astronauts do.) There's no food on the moon, either. Nothing grows—not even weeds.

If the man on the moon liked to climb mountains, he would be very happy. There are many high places there, such as the tall rims around the holes, or *craters*, of the moon. Some of these rims are as tall as Earth's highest mountains.

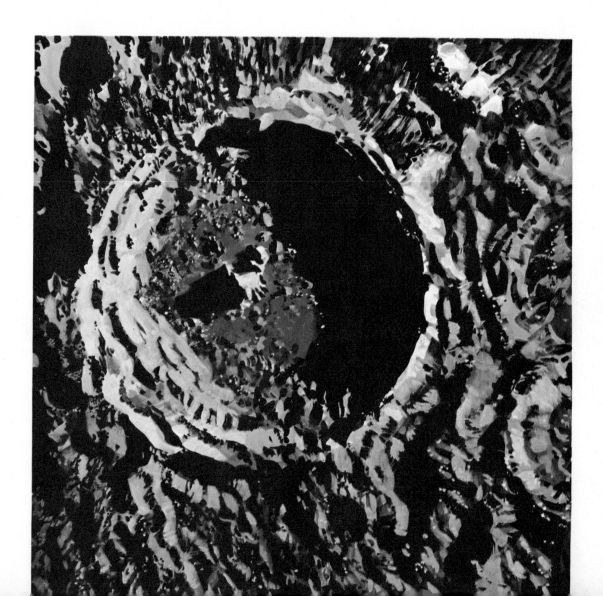

But if the man on the moon liked to swim, he would be unhappy. There is no water on the moon—just dust and rock.

When you think of what it's like on the moon, you may wonder why it interests our scientists. One reason is that the moon is Earth's nearest neighbor—it is the easiest place in space to get to.

Going back and forth between the moon and Earth, astronauts will get a lot of practice in space travel. Things learned on moon trips will be of great help to astronauts who later take long, long trips to some of the planets.

Scientists are also interested in the moon because it has no air. The air that surrounds Earth cuts down the view of the scientists who look at the stars through telescopes. A telescope on the moon would give them a clearer, closer view of the stars.

The World's Worst Sound

M-m-m-m-m-m-s-s-z-z-sz-sz- n-n-z-z-zing-ing-ing!

Can you make a sound like a mosquito about to bite you?

Some people think a mosquito's hum is the worst sound in the world.

Do you know *anybody* who is a friend to a mosquito?

If you could tell the difference between a mother mosquito and a father mosquito, you might at least be a friend to the father mosquitoes. It is only the mother mosquitoes that bite and leave those itchy lumps on your arms or legs. The father mosquitoes seem to be satisfied with a meal of nectar and plant juices.

A mosquito doesn't make its humming sound with its mouth, as you may suppose. The sound you hear when a mosquito is near your ear comes from the fast beat of the mosquito's wings.

Mosquitoes are usually found wherever the weather is damp or where there are rivers or lakes or swamps. Far north toward the North Pole in summer, there are so many mosquitoes that together they look like black clouds. Sometimes mosquitoes are so high up in the air that they even get in through the open windows of tall apartment buildings in New York City.

Mosquitoes lay their eggs in water—in ponds, in ditches, or sometimes in tin cans that are partly filled with rainwater.

Baby mosquitoes are not babies for very long. When the eggs are first hatched, the baby mosquitoes have no wings. They live in the water and are called *wrigglers,* probably because their long, thin bodies wriggle around so much.

They grow very fast. There is one kind that grows from an egg to a full-grown mosquito in seven days. Just think of that—growing up in one week!

Trying to get rid of mosquitoes is a long, hard battle. One way to fight them is to drain all the water out of ditches and swamps and ponds where they lay their eggs.

Sometimes oil is poured on top of the water to destroy the mosquitoes that are still wrigglers. They can't breathe because of the oil, and they can't fly away because their wings haven't grown yet.

To destroy full-grown mosquitoes, different kinds of *insecticides* are used. An insecticide is a powder or liquid for killing harmful insects. These are sometimes sprayed as a poisonous fog from trucks.

Great care must be taken in the use of the sprays, or they will kill other things that shouldn't be killed.

There are other liquids, called *repellents*, that people can rub or spray on their skin to keep mosquitoes from biting them.

One of the nicest ways to get rid of mosquitoes is to build a purple-martin house. Purple martins are birds that catch mosquitoes in the air and eat them.

How Did the Mountains Get There?

George Hunter—Publix Pictorial

In some places the ground is flat as far as you can see.
Is it that way where you live?

In other places hills go up and down all around—hills of great humped mountains covered with forests. On even higher mountains bare rock goes up and up, like the walls of a giant's house. These mountains are so high they poke above the clouds.

What makes mountains? Where did all these mountains come from in the first place?

Bernie Donahue—Publix Pictorial

234

In the beginning, before there were people or trees—even before there were dinosaurs—the Earth was a hot and fiery place. Much too hot for anything to live on it.

Slowly, slowly it became cool. On the outside. But on the inside it stayed hot. In some places, bubbling hot.

Here and there some of the hot melted rock pushed outside through cracks and holes in the earth. As this rock cooled, it became hard and solid. But more hot melted rock, or *lava,* as it is called, poured out on top of the hard rock. As it cooled, it became hard, too. This kept happening, and the hard rock built up higher and higher—until there was a mountain!

235

Mountains were formed in other ways, too.

In those faraway days when the Earth was new, there were more earthquakes than there are now. Sometimes there would be an earthquake so strong that the rock on top for miles and miles would break and turn on edge. Part of the earth would then be lower and part of it higher. Earthquakes might keep happening, moving the rock around under the ground and pushing the rock on top higher and higher—high enough to make more mountains.

Some of the biggest mountains in the world, such as the Alps and the Rocky Mountains, were pushed up from the bottom of oceans that were in the world long ago.

We don't know for sure what pushed them up, because nobody was there to look inside the Earth. But if you put your hands on two sides of some wet sand or mud, and then push your hands together slowly, you would see how the sand or mud rises up between your hands. And that is the way it seems that some of our biggest mountains came up—with the rocks all wrinkled and folded—as if they had been pushed by other rocks from each side.

237

Grant Heilm

At first most of the mountains on Earth were steep and sharp. But the wind blew and the rain fell for millions and millions of years—more years than you can count. Even hard rocks can be worn away if you rub at them long enough. Slowly, slowly, with the wind and the rain rubbing at them, the steep, sharp mountains grew smoother and shorter and rounder.

After many, many years a mountain wears down and becomes not so steep and tall. It is easy to tell today which of the mountains have been here the longest time. They are the mountains

Grant Heilmar

that are *not* so high. The wind and the rain have worked on them for so long that now their slopes are gentle. They are so low that trees grow on top of many of them.

The newest mountains are still steep and high.

The *very* newest mountains are still being made, as once in a while a new volcano starts somewhere on Earth.

Why Animals and Plants Live Where They Do

This raccoon is hungry. He is watching the fish just a few inches away in the brook.

Suddenly the raccoon's paw scoops into the water and—*splash!* His paw has moved fast, but not fast enough this time—the fish gets away.

The raccoon and the fish can live just inches away from each other—but the raccoon can never live under the water, and the fish cannot live out in the air.

Every kind of plant or animal on Earth has certain places where it can live and others where it cannot. It's easy to understand why a raccoon can't live underwater and why a fish can't live out of the water. Each one breathes in a different way.

But there are many other reasons that some plants and animals live where they do. Certain men study these reasons in a science called *ecology*.

As a group of plants or animals grows larger, it spreads out. Finally it may come to a river, an ocean, or a high mountain. For a long time then, or maybe forever, these plants or animals will be found on one side of the barrier but not on the other side.

If an animal eats only certain kinds of plants, you'll find that animal only where those plants grow. The eucalyptus leaves that koala bears eat grow in Australia. So that's where koalas live. When koalas are taken away from Australia to live in a zoo, a supply of special leaves is kept on hand for the koalas' dinner.

In any particular place on Earth there is only so much food, water, and space. If two kinds of plants or animals want the same food or water or space they will both try to get it.

One kind may be able to push the other out and get all of the food, water, or space for itself. Or they may each take what they can and live together in the same space.

Plants and animals that live in parts of the world where it is very hot usually cannot live where it is very cold. And animals from cold places usually cannot live where it is very hot.

To grow, most plants need dirt that is rich in certain foods. If the ground is very sandy or is made of solid rock, most plants will not be found there. But a few plants that like a lot of sunshine and don't need much water or chemical food are found in such sandy or rocky places. These special plants are often not found anywhere else because other plants would crowd them out or block them from the sunshine.

Sometimes the things that keep a plant or animal in one place are not so easy to see.

The brown pelican, for example, feeds on fish, so you might think he could live well near any of the oceans. But he can't.

This pelican gets his food in a special way. He flies high over the ocean until he spots a fish in the water below. Then he dives into the clear water and catches the fish.

Because of this unusual way of getting food, a brown pelican that lives in the clear waters of the Caribbean Sea has been able to spread out only as far as the very clear waters go. If he tried to move farther he would not be able to see the fish that he depends upon for food.

Another bird called the Arctic tern does not breed near the Bering Sea. For a long time scientists could not figure out why this was so.

Then they discovered that during the time when the chicks must be fed they gain weight on fair days but lose weight on foggy days—at least they don't find food then.

Scientists believe that the many foggy days near the Bering Sea keep the Arctic tern from breeding there.

Sometimes we find a plant or animal living in a place where nothing else can grow.

The red mangrove tree can grow in salty, muddy water along warm seacoasts. Before the seeds fall from the mangrove tree each seed grows a root. When the seed falls, the root may be pushed into the mud, or sometimes the root grows down into the mud before the seed falls.

The mangrove tree grows quickly, and its roots branch out and make a trap that catches mud and driftwood floating in the water. These things collect and build up solid ground.

Because the mangrove tree can grow in such an unlikely place, it has the space where it grows pretty much to itself.

However, we all know that there is one animal that is intelligent enough to figure out how to make houses and clothing. He can grow food and take it with him wherever he goes. This animal is called *man* and he can live almost any place on Earth that he wishes.

The World of Water

If you live in the middle of a big country, you may never have seen much water. You may find it hard to believe that much more than half the Earth is covered by water.

If you live on a small island in the middle of the ocean, you may find it hard to believe that so much of the Earth is land.

But if you were an astronaut circling high above the Earth, you'd see that there is more water than land. You'd see with your very own eyes how the land and the water are divided.

The next best thing to being an astronaut is pretending to be one when you're looking at a globe.

A globe is a world map that's round—more perfectly round than the world is. You see lots of blue on the globe. The blue is for water, and the green is for land. Big chunks of land divide the blue. These big chunks look like pieces from a giant jigsaw puzzle. These big pieces of land are called *continents*. The waters around the continents are called *oceans*.

The continents have names. So do the oceans.

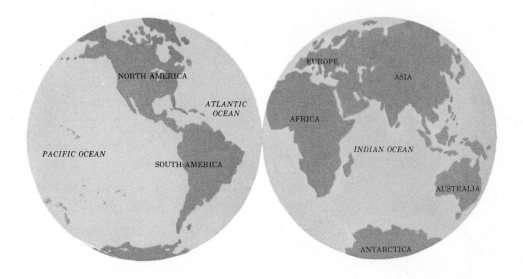

Which continent do you live on? Which oceans are near your continent?

Even though most of the land on Earth has been explored, you can still become an explorer under the ocean. To help learn more about the deep, dark, silent, underwater world, scientists have made machines to send back echoes from the bottom of the ocean. Scientists use the echoes to figure out how deep it is without going down there to find out.

But it's also possible to go down to the bottom.

People can go down inside a metal ball called a *bathysphere*. They can look through windows to watch fish and other ocean creatures. Some bathyspheres even have a door so that people can step outside, breathing from a tank of air, and go walking on the ocean floor.

If people want to go still deeper under the ocean, they can go in a *bathyscaphe*. This is a special kind of submarine that can move around and explore the ocean in very deep places.

People used to think that the bottoms of the oceans were just about as smooth and flat as the bottom of a swimming pool. But now we know that under the oceans there are plains and valleys, mountains and canyons. Some of the mountains are even higher, and some of the canyons deeper, than any on the land. Every year we are learning more about the ocean floor, and we are making maps of it.

Far under the ocean everything looks dark and still. On top the water never stops moving. Sun shines on it and makes it

sparkle. Its blue green colors seem to change with the curl and lift of every wave. The ocean breezes make you feel cool and clean. The sounds of the water gently splashing on the shore or crashing against great rocks are as much fun to listen to as a thousand tunes. And there's the fresh salty air of the sea to smell and taste while you run and splash in the waves at the seashore.

Because of the oceans, you have a better life wherever you are—even if you live too far from the ocean to spend a day at the beach. The oceans provide food for you. They are broad highways for ships that bring useful and beautiful things from many other lands. The waters of the oceans add moisture to the air—the air makes clouds—the clouds make rain—the rain keeps your plants blooming.

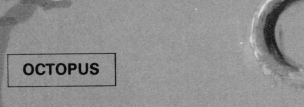

The Many-Armed Wonder

If you had eight arms that you could use for legs—or eight legs that you could use for arms . . .

And if your eyes stuck out at the top of your arms—or legs . . .

And if you had a big head that flopped over like a bag when you rested . . .

If you had practically no neck . . .

If your mouth were underneath your head . . .

If you could change your color whenever you wanted to . . .

If you lived in ocean water and laid eggs and could squirt out a kind of black ink that made the water cloudy so that no animal could see you . . .

Do you know what people would call you?

They'd call you an *octopus*.

Not so many years ago, people told wild stories about a deep-sea monster that came up from the bottom of the ocean and wrapped long, wriggling arms around a big ship and dragged it under the water. They called this monster a devilfish or octopus.

But now we know that no octopus grows so large. Some of them are no bigger than your hand. Most of them are no bigger than a man and are not even mean or dangerous. They are shy creatures that eat shellfish, such as crabs, lobsters, and mussels. They swim or run away fast across the sea bottom on their eight rubbery arms—or legs—if you try to come close.

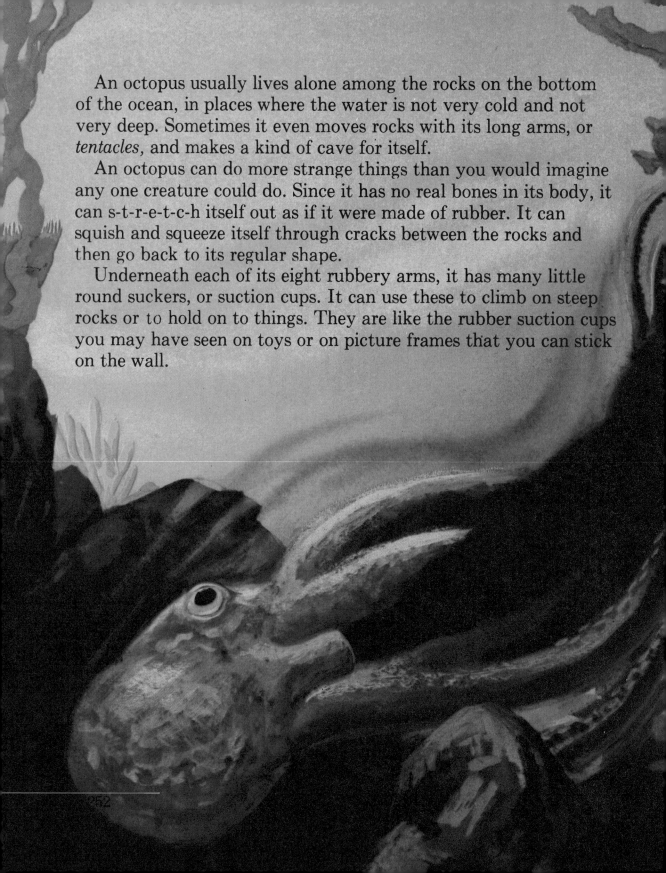

An octopus usually lives alone among the rocks on the bottom of the ocean, in places where the water is not very cold and not very deep. Sometimes it even moves rocks with its long arms, or *tentacles,* and makes a kind of cave for itself.

An octopus can do more strange things than you would imagine any one creature could do. Since it has no real bones in its body, it can s-t-r-e-t-c-h itself out as if it were made of rubber. It can squish and squeeze itself through cracks between the rocks and then go back to its regular shape.

Underneath each of its eight rubbery arms, it has many little round suckers, or suction cups. It can use these to climb on steep rocks or to hold on to things. They are like the rubber suction cups you may have seen on toys or on picture frames that you can stick on the wall.

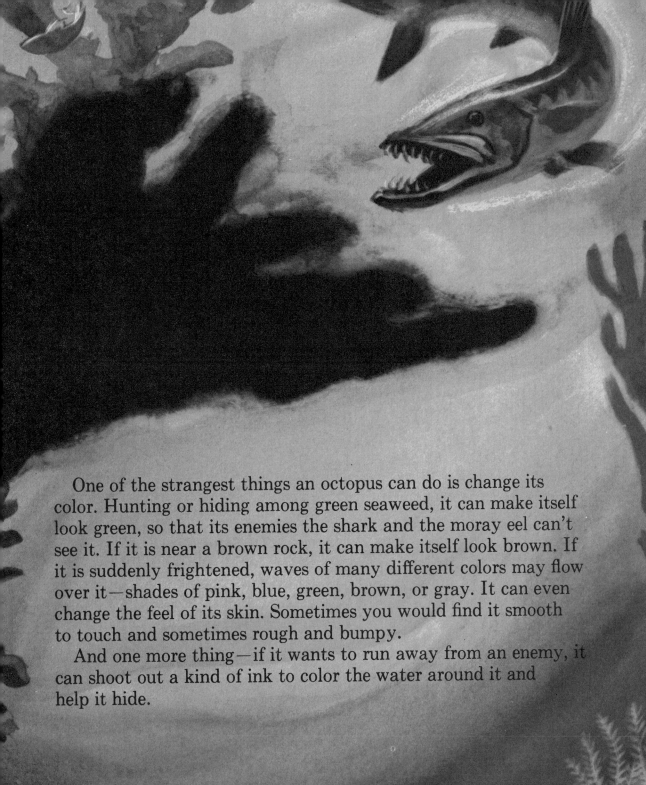

One of the strangest things an octopus can do is change its color. Hunting or hiding among green seaweed, it can make itself look green, so that its enemies the shark and the moray eel can't see it. If it is near a brown rock, it can make itself look brown. If it is suddenly frightened, waves of many different colors may flow over it—shades of pink, blue, green, brown, or gray. It can even change the feel of its skin. Sometimes you would find it smooth to touch and sometimes rough and bumpy.

And one more thing—if it wants to run away from an enemy, it can shoot out a kind of ink to color the water around it and help it hide.

The Bird in the Swinging Nest

It's springtime. All the birds are building nests.

But what is this bird doing? It's a mother oriole, and she's building a nest, too! But it won't be an ordinary nest—a little bowl of mud and twigs and grass perched on a tree limb. To build *her* nest, the mother oriole hangs upside down from a high tree limb, holding a long piece of string in her beak. With this and other pieces of string and grass, she weaves a long sack that will sway gently in the wind.

The oriole usually fastens her fancy nest in a tree at a place where two branches come together. This leaves plenty of room for the birds to get into the nest from the open top.

Once the long sides of the hanging nest are made, the mother oriole stands over the top, balancing herself with spread wings, while she sticks her head inside the sack nest and weaves the bottom.

It takes her about six days to make this remarkable nest.

254

What do you suppose the father oriole is doing all this time?
Not very much. He lets Mamma do all the work, while he struts
back and forth on the limb, showing the world his pretty orange
and black feathers.

But now it's time for him to work, too.

He crawls inside the new sack and begins fluttering his wings,
making all kinds of noise and shaking the branches. His fast-
moving wings widen and shape the nest so that there will be room
for the eggs the mother oriole is going to lay.

The mother oriole finishes the nest by putting soft pieces of moss and rags in the bottom.

After the baby orioles are hatched from the eggs, they are safe and warm in their sack home. Even the rough winds of a spring storm can't harm them. Their home just swings back and forth while they sleep inside.

Orioles nest in the same tree year after year. If you see orioles nesting in a tree near your house or in a park, you should look for the same birds again next spring.

The Biggest Bird in the World

What if you looked out the window and saw a bird as tall as a tree?

You'd surely be surprised. Maybe even frightened. Of course, there aren't any birds that large anymore. But thousands of years ago, there really were giant birds. One was so enormous that it is called an *elephant bird.*

What if you looked out the window and saw an ostrich? You'd probably be surprised, but you wouldn't need to be afraid. The ostrich is usually quite gentle.

And it is the biggest living bird in the whole world today. The very *biggest!*

Ostriches are so big and so heavy and their wings so short that they can't fly. But they can run faster than any other bird— almost as fast as a horse. To help them go faster, they flap their wings when they run. Sometimes they roam in large herds in the desert or on the grassy plains.

People used to say that an ostrich was a foolish bird. They thought it buried its head in the sand when it was in danger. They said that when an ostrich could not see its enemies, it thought its enemies could not see it.

But this isn't true about the ostrich. When it has its head down like that, it is looking for berries and seeds to eat.

It fights with its beak and especially with its feet. Don't stand close to an ostrich if it is angry. It can kick like a mule! But if you are kind to an ostrich and treat it well, it may become so tame that it will carry you around on its back.

Diving and Swimming Champ

Floating lazily on its back—rocking in the icy ocean waves—this otter might seem just to be taking a nap.

Not true! If you look closely, you'll see this furry fellow is hard at work getting the tasty meat out of a clamshell.

A strange way to eat, lying on your back! But that's how sea otters often do it. They use their front paws as hands, and their stomachs for tables!

Most amazing of all, the sea otter sometimes uses a stone to help it get food. It is one of the few animals smart enough to use a tool. This diving sea otter didn't go to the ocean bottom only to gather clams. While it was down there, it picked up a stone to use in cracking open the clamshells!

An otter's big webbed feet are just right for swimming and diving deep under the water. Otters are among the fastest-swimming animals.

When night comes, this clever fisherman likes to wrap itself in some giant seaweed near shore. The weeds make a soft nest for sleeping and also help keep the otter safe from dangerous sharks.

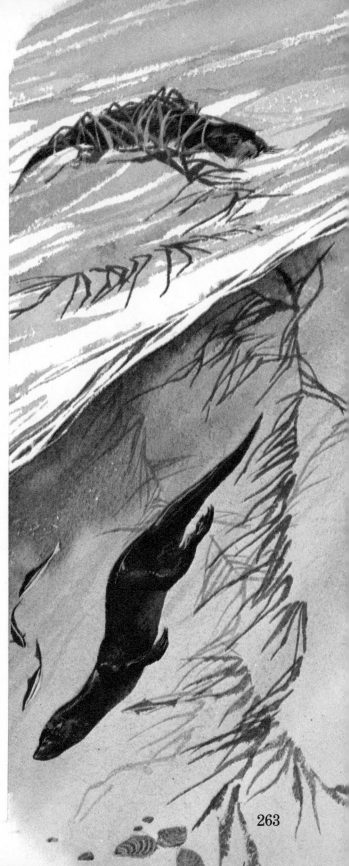

If you should see a whiskery, shiny animal with a long, skinny body sliding down a muddy bank into a river—*splash*—it would look like a sea otter. But it isn't.

It's a river otter. Playful and funny, it makes a delightful pet.

River otters are champion swimmers, too. The river otter knows just how to build a nest lined with leaves and grass—not in water but under the ground—in a tunnel that it digs near a river or a lake.

Sometimes the nest will be buried under the roots of a tree. But no matter where the nest is, it's warm and safe for the whole family.

Baby otters don't know how to swim when they're born. The babies that are afraid of the water are carried on their mother's back until they're ready to take off on their own. Then they dive for good things to eat—fish, frogs, snails, and shellfish.

The Owl at Night

The owl is a bird that flies at night. Because of its very soft feathers, it flies as silently as a breeze, swooping down on mice, gophers, rats, and sometimes even on such large animals as rabbits and squirrels and skunks.

It catches them in its long, strong claws. In a single night some owls can eat their own weight in mice and rats.

Owls are big. Owls are little. Some are as big as a fireplug. Some are so small that they would fit in your pocket. But don't try to put one there, or you'll get scratched and bitten!

North, south, east, and west—owls live almost everywhere. Some live in forests or parks, probably close to where you live— maybe even in your own backyard. Listen, and you might hear one at night. Some owls make beautiful, sad music.

Owls can see better at night than most animals, and they hunt for their food in the dusk and dark. They sleep during the day, hidden away among the tree branches.

If you found an owl in the daytime sitting on a tree branch, you might think at first it wasn't real. It would probably just sit there not moving a feather. It wouldn't even move its eyes. It *couldn't* because an owl's eyes can't move.

The only way an owl can look around is to turn its head. But it can turn its head almost all the way around. And it can turn it so fast that you can hardly see it move.

People say owls make sounds of *whoo-whoo-whoo,* and some do.

But owls also make sounds like those of other animals:

Some meow like a kitten, yap like a puppy, or hiss like a snake.

Sometimes when owls make their sounds, they frighten the animals they're hunting. The animals give themselves away by running. Then the owls catch them.

Some people say owls are wise, but there is no proof that owls are smarter than any other birds.

PEANUTS

The Crunchy Treat

270
ZIBEL

What's in this picture?

They *look* like peanuts.

They have shells like peanuts, and they have skins like peanuts.

They *look* like peanuts, and they *taste* like peanuts.

They *are* peanuts.

But *they're not nuts*.

No one picked them from a tree or a bush or shook them from the branches. Someone dug them up out of the ground, where they grew like potatoes or beets or carrots.

Although they look and taste like nuts and everybody calls them nuts, peanuts are really a kind of pea—a pea that grows under the ground. When you think about it, they do look a *little* like peas in a pod. But the peanut pod is a spongy shell, covered with tiny dimples. The shell is narrow in the middle, as if someone had tied a string tightly around it.

You don't need a nutcracker to break the shell. You can break it with your fingers. Inside the shell you will usually find two peanuts. But sometimes there is only one. And once in a while there may be four or five.

Peanuts grow easily in warm, sandy places. Their vines grow as high as, or maybe a little higher than, your knees. And they have golden yellow flowers.

When the peanuts are ripe, the plants are dug up and stacked against sticks to dry out. After the peanuts are picked, the tops of the dry plants are used as hay for animals.

Peanuts are usually roasted in their shells before they are eaten. Or they are shelled and prepared as salted peanuts or as peanut butter.

When creamy peanut butter is spread on a piece of bread or toast, it doesn't look much like peanuts, but it still tastes peanutty. In some parts of the world, peanuts are grown just for their oil.

And what would a circus be without any peanuts to feed the elephants—and you?

The Most Unusual Birds

If there were a contest for the most unusual bird, the penguin might win the prize.

Of course, the ostrich has a strange long neck, and the peacock has beautiful tail feathers, which it can spread out like a fan.

The heron sleeps standing on one leg, and the pelican has a lower bill so huge it can hold a whole big fish. Hummingbirds can stay still in the air with their wings going so fast you can't see them move. And woodpeckers have beaks so strong and pointed they can drill a hole in a tree—or even a house.

There is something unusual about the way each of these birds looks or acts.

But what would the contest judges think about a bird that
    couldn't fly,
    could swim through icy water as fast as a motorboat,
    could swim along, dive 30 feet under the water, and then
come up so fast it would zip out of the water high enough to jump
over a wall,
    and would build a nest out of stones instead of twigs and
grass?

They'd think this bird—called
a *penguin*—was a very unusual
bird.

Almost anything that penguins do, they do in an unusual way.

Some baby penguins are born at the very cold South Pole during the long winter, when it is dark for many, many days. As soon as the egg has been laid, the mother penguin walks back to the ocean.

The father penguin stays and balances the egg on his feet. A flap on his belly keeps the egg warm. He waits until the mother penguin returns, which is about the same time that the egg hatches.

She feeds the gray fluffy baby penguin from her beak.

Now it is the father penguin's turn to look for food.

The penguin's feathers are very tiny and close together all over its body. This helps keep it warm.

When it swims, its light-colored belly and dark-colored back help hide it from enemies. From underneath in the water, its light belly makes it hard for the leopard seal to see it. From above, its dark back looks like the dark water, helping to hide it from big hunting birds.

One kind of penguin makes its nest out of rocks. Another lays one big egg and one little one. But only the big one hatches into a chick. So no one knows why the penguin lays the little egg.

Now would you be surprised if the penguin won the contest for the most unusual bird?

Why Things Grow

Why do trees and other plants grow in some places and not in others? Why does some land have so much growing on it, while other land has almost no plants growing on it at all?

To grow, plants need several things. One is warmth. In very cold places almost nothing grows. That's why the cold land at the North and the South Poles is so bare.

Plants also need water. In very dry parts of the Earth only a few unusual plants can grow. That's why dry deserts everywhere are almost bare.

Plants must also have a place in which to put down their roots and grow. They find it hard to grow on rocky land.

This town is built on rocky land. The plants here have only the soil found between the cracks of the rocks to grow in.

Even where there are no rocks, the soil must be loose enough for the roots to push their way down and for the air and water to find their way to the roots. That is why farmers plow their fields—to loosen the soil.

Another thing plants must have before they can grow is food.

What would happen if we tried to make things grow on this sandy beach? A few plants, such as beach grass, will grow in sand, but most plants won't. Even if the weather was warm enough and we watered the plants each day, many of them would die because the sand on this beach has very little food for plants.

What kind of food do plants need?

They need the kind that is in soil where other plants have grown and died. When plants die, the sun dries them up. Then wind and rain break them into little powdery pieces, and they become part of the soil—an important part that will feed new plants.

When soil holds a lot of this kind of food and there is enough warmth and water, plants of many kinds grow thick and green.

While growing, plants use up the food in the soil. The food that these cabbages took from the soil won't go back into it because the cabbages will be taken away to be eaten. What happens then?

The farmer has to put new food for plants into the soil. Sometimes he does this by planting a different kind of growing thing and then later plowing it under the soil. Or he may let the land rest for a year or two. But more often he puts a plant food called *fertilizer* into the soil. He buys the fertilizer in bags or tanks and uses a machine to sprinkle or spray it evenly onto the land. The fertilizer gives back to the land some of the plant food that growing plants took out of it.

Insects, Watch Out!

This plant growing at the edge of a pond *looks* harmless enough. But it isn't—not for this fly.

If the fly smells the sweet-smelling nectar in this plant and touches a leaf, it will be captured.

Just brushing against one tiny hair on the edge of the leaf will make the plant snap shut—with the fly trapped inside!

The plant is called a *Venus's-flytrap*.

It catches insects and eats them!

To stay alive, most plants get all the things they need from the soil they grow in and from the air and the sun. But this plant seems to need other things as well. It gets them by trapping insects.

Of course, these plants don't really eat food the way you do. They can't chew or swallow. They simply soak up the good parts of the insect to use for food.

Have you ever had a plant for a pet? Well, a Venus's-flytrap is no ordinary pet. But you can buy one in a plant store, keep it at home, and watch how it traps food. If you do buy one, be sure to ask about instructions for taking care of it!

A Venus's-flytrap isn't the only plant that captures insects. This pitcher plant has leaves shaped like small pitchers. But it doesn't trap food by snapping its leaves shut. Instead, its leaves have slippery insides—so slippery that when an insect climbs in to taste the nectar, it slips and slides all the way to the bottom of the leaf.

Most insect-eating plants grow near damp or wet places. This bladderwort is one that lives right *in* water—floating on top or growing on the bottom of a muddy pond or swamp.

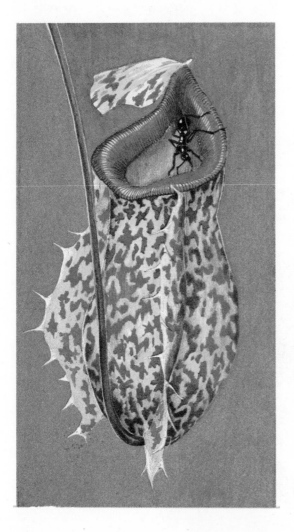 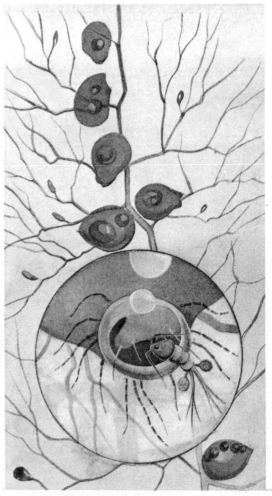

It catches tiny water creatures with a trap no bigger than the tip of your finger. The trap is shaped like a very small bag and has bristles growing around an opening. When a water insect touches one of the bristles, the bag opens and traps the insect for food.

The skinny stalks covering the leaf of the sundew plant are coated with a sticky liquid—just right for catching food. When the sun shines, the sundew plant shines, too. Insects easily find their way onto the sticky stalks. But getting away isn't easy at all. The harder an insect tries to crawl off the stalk, the more it gets stuck.

Some people believe there are plants big enough to eat people! But there aren't any that big. No plants eat people. They *really* don't. And about the only ones that eat insects are the plants pictured here.

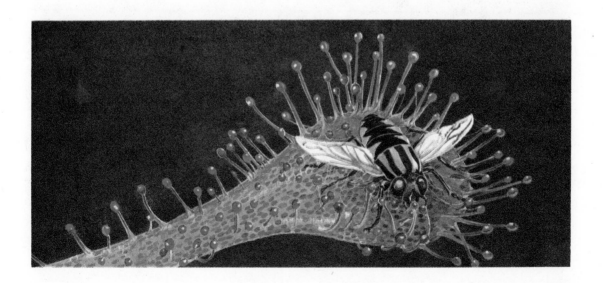

Long Ears and Big Eyes

Rabbits have things that keep them safe—
Long ears for hearing the slightest sound,
Sharp claws for digging a nest in the ground,
Big eyes for looking to see what's around,
Strong legs for running, in case they are found.

The kind of rabbit you're most likely to see has a little white nub of a tail, like a fluff of cotton. That's why it's called a *cotton-tail rabbit*.

The mother rabbit is gentle when she's taking care of her babies. Before they're born, she builds a soft padded nest in a hollow scraped out under the grass, or in a burrow between the big roots of a tree.

She carefully shreds leaves and collects grass for a nest lining. Then she pulls bits of fur from her thick coat to make a warm, snug bed. Baby rabbits can't see at first. And they haven't any fur. So the mother never leaves the nest without covering it with more leaves and grass to keep her babies safe.

Rabbit mothers aren't gentle when their babies are in danger from other animals—such as dogs, foxes, snakes, owls, or hawks. They kick hard with their feet. And they bite!

Jackrabbits and snowshoe rabbits don't build nests. Their homes are flat places in the grass under trees or in brush heaps. Their babies have fur and can see from birth.

But then, they aren't rabbits. They're *called* rabbits. They look like rabbits. But they're *hares*. They're bigger and fatter. Their ears are longer. Their legs are so much longer they could jump across a big living room in one jump . . . which is about twice as far as a rabbit can jump!

Snowshoe rabbits turn white in the winter, so their enemies can't easily find them in the snow.

Both rabbits and hares hunt for food at night—juicy green plants and crops in warm weather, berries and bark from trees in the winter. They hide during the day. And if you've heard the story about the rabbit jumping into a thorny bush to stay safe . . . it's true. They make twisting paths through thorny under-brush where their enemies can't follow.

Sweets from the Sun

Hold a raisin in your hand and look at it. Where did it come from? Did a machine make it? Is it part of an animal? Did it grow on a tree?

Here's a riddle: *When is a raisin not a raisin?*

Answer: *When it is a grape.*

A raisin starts out as a grape. In California and other sunny places in the world, a grape hangs on a vine in a bunch with many other grapes. Under the hot summer sun it grows fat and round and juicy.

Some of the grapes are picked and placed on a wooden tray where the sun shines on them day after day. Slowly the sun dries up the water that is in the grape. The grape becomes wrinkled. It turns blackish brown and becomes a raisin.

Finally a workman comes by in a truck, picks up all the raisins, and takes them to a packing plant.

At the packing plant the stems are taken off by machines, and the raisins are washed. After drying again, they are packed in boxes and shipped to stores all over the world.

There is something else with a life story very much like a raisin's. That's a prune, which is wrinkled and dark brown like a raisin, only bigger.

Here's another riddle: *When is a prune not a prune?*

Answer: *When it is a plum!*

The Teeth That Keep On Growing

Who made the hole in the wall?

This mouse did.

What did it use for a tool?

Its front teeth.

Mice are *rodents*, and rodents are *gnawers*. The name rodent comes from a Latin word that means "to gnaw." And to gnaw means "to bite and nibble." Rodents have front teeth that are very good for gnawing. This mouse just gnawed a front door for his home inside the wall.

Many different animals have these special teeth that are so good for gnawing. Woodchucks, gophers, chipmunks, rats, prairie dogs, and squirrels are all rodents.

Your teeth grow to a certain size, and then they stop growing. But a rodent's two front top teeth and its two front bottom teeth keep growing as long as it lives. It's a good thing they do.

Rodents gnaw their food, and as the nuts, roots, seeds, or leaves are ground into pieces, the part of the tooth doing the grinding is rubbed so hard that some of it is ground away.

If these teeth didn't keep growing, the grinding would soon make the teeth too short. And growing without the grinding would make them too long!

So the growing and the grinding work together to keep the rodents' teeth a good length for the things they have to do.

Rubber Trees

If all the things made of rubber in this picture suddenly disappeared . . .

No balloons! No ball to bounce! No boots! And the truck couldn't move very far without tires.

This tall thin tree with smooth bark is a rubber tree. It grows in a small forest on a rubber plantation in Malaysia where the weather is hot and rainy.

This woman is collecting the milky liquid the rubber will be made from.

After the buckets are full, the juice is taken to a factory where it is poured into pans to dry and thicken.

292

Then it's pressed through rollers,
hung in sheets to dry some more,
tied in big bundles,
and shipped to factories where it is made into tires, balloons,
boots, rubber bands, pencil erasers, and hundreds of other things
we use every day.

Lots of the things you use that seem to be made of rubber are really made of synthetic rubber. Instead of coming from a tree, this rubbery stuff is made in a factory.

Sand Everywhere

Sand.

Sand everywhere.

Sand down your neck, and sand between your toes.

Sand at the seashore. You can see it along the beach in two directions as far as you can look.

Sand in the desert. There you can see sand in *four* directions as far as you can look.

There is sand at the bottoms of rivers, sand piled up in hills, or *dunes,* at the edge of lakes, sand in mountain valleys, and sand under the earth and on top of the earth almost anywhere.

It wasn't always there. Where did it come from?

Most things start small and grow big. But sand starts big and grows small, though *grow* isn't exactly the right word. Sand doesn't *grow* small. It becomes that way when bigger things, mostly rocks, break into smaller pieces.

The wind, the frost, and the rain are great sand-makers. They work against high mountain cliffs . . . and slowly . . . slowly . . . through millions of years . . . they break off pieces of rock, which tumble down the mountainside. As the rock bangs and bounces, it breaks off other pieces of rock, at the same time breaking itself into smaller pieces. It isn't sand yet, but it's starting to be.

Rivers help make sand, too. The water of a river rushes down the mountainside, rolling rocks along and breaking them into smaller and smaller pieces. Glaciers are another good sand-maker. The heavy ice scrapes and grinds the rocks that it moves across. The ice also carries along the sand it has made and dumps it in places far away.

Another great sand-maker is the ocean. All over the world the tides rise and fall, and storm waves tear at the rocks along the shore, banging them together, wearing them down . . . until finally some of the rocks are so small that they are what we call *sand*.

Most brown sand comes from a hard mineral called *quartz*, mixed with broken rocks. White sand comes from coral and seashells that have been broken up by the wind and water. Lava, which flows from volcanoes, is often broken up into black sand. There are also red, gray, and green sands. There is even golden sand—specks of real gold—which sometimes collects at the bottoms of fast-moving streams.

Water Clowns

These rocks at the edge of San Francisco's beach are known all over the world. People come from far away to see them. Or really to see the brown animals that live on them.

People say, "Oh, *there* they are! Listen to them barking!"

The animals do sound something like dogs. But they are fur-covered seals. Well . . . people *call* them seals, and these rocks are known everywhere as Seal Rocks, but the animals really are *sea lions*.

There are many other rocks along the coast where sea lions live, but these are the most famous ones.

You can tell the difference between seals and sea lions by their ears. True seals have no outside ears, just tiny holes to hear through. Sea lions have small outside ears.

Seals and sea lions have finned flippers instead of feet. They are land-and-water animals. Their food is mostly fish, squid, and shellfish, and they swallow it whole.

Swimming in the water, seals are swift and graceful. But on land they go flip-flopping along on their flippers with an awkward waddle.

Seals and sea lions sleep on land, and their babies, or *pups,* as they are called, are born on land. When it's time to learn to swim, a mother picks up her pup by the back of its neck, just as a mother cat picks up a kitten. Then she carries it to the water for its first swimming lesson. After a few weeks, a group of baby seals will go into the water and dive and play like children.

The trained seals in circuses and zoos are really the seals with outside ears—the California sea lions. They are very smart and love to play and are easily trained to do tricks. A sea lion can be taught to balance a big rubber ball on the end of its nose or play a tune on a row of trumpets. *You* might play the trumpets, but could you balance the ball?

Sea lions like the way people clap their hands after a trick. Sometimes sea lions even applaud themselves by clapping their front flippers together!

What sea lions like most of all is fish. So every time a sea lion does a trick, its trainer tosses it a piece of fish. The idea seems to be—do a trick, get a fish.

There are more seals in the cold, frozen Far North than in any
other place. These are the fur seals, the true seals with no outside
ears. Their coats are thick and beautiful, and underneath they
have a layer of *blubber,* or fat, to keep them warm.

The small harbor seals live along reefs and coastal islands or in
lakes. Though shy, they like company, and if you are friendly,
they will be friendly, too.

Harbor seals make good pets, but maybe not house
pets. Your father might not like one in his favorite
chair! And what would your mother say if it
flopped its muddy flippers over her clean rug?

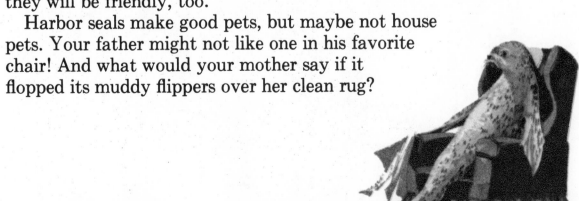

Seeds That Fly

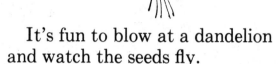

Puff!

He's blowing at a fluffy dandelion—and soon hundreds of new dandelion plants may begin to grow.

It's fun to blow at a dandelion and watch the seeds fly.

Usually a gust of wind sweeps the dandelion seeds off the plant and into the air. Low and high, they dip and fly until they drop softly to the ground.

If a seed lands in a place that's good for growing, and if there's just the right amount of rain and sunshine needed for that kind of seed, then one day it may become a new dandelion plant.

A *seed* is the part of a plant from which a new plant grows. The seed can be as small as a speck of dust or as big as a coconut.

Inside each dandelion seed is a tiny
plant and a bit of plant food.

And on the outside there's a covering called a *seed coat*. The seed coat
protects everything that's inside.

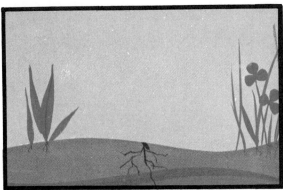

When the seed starts to grow, a tiny
point pushes down into the ground.
That's the *root*.

Then another little shoot pushes up
into the air. That's the *stem*.

Dandelion seeds are not the only seeds that fly with the breezes.

The two-winged seeds of a maple tree spin and twirl to the ground like toy propellers.

From just one maple tree, thousands and thousands of seeds will fall and whirl.

Many of the seeds that fall do not grow into plants. Animals eat many of them. Bears, beavers, chipmunks, and squirrels feast on them. Hungry little mice and big rats, too, devour seeds. Birds gobble them up.

Many seeds land in places where they can't grow.

Some seeds float on water.

Other seeds are caught in animal fur and may be carried for miles.

Pine seeds drop from pine cones and glide through the air. They fall to the ground slowly, on just one wing.

The spurting cucumber *pops* its seeds into the air.

Animals That Live in Shells

There are many different shelled animals. The smallest live in shells as tiny as the letter *o*. The largest are found in the ocean near Australia and weigh nearly 600 pounds!

There have been times when a pearl diver has accidentally put his arm into the open shell of a giant clam. The clam tried to close its shell, to protect itself, and caught the diver. Because of accidents like that, this giant shelled animal is sometimes called the *man-eating clam*.

Some shells are all in one piece. They are called *univalves*. Other shells are made up of two pieces that are the same size and fit together perfectly. A hinge holds the two-piece shell together. These shells are called *bivalves*.

What do these shells look like to you?

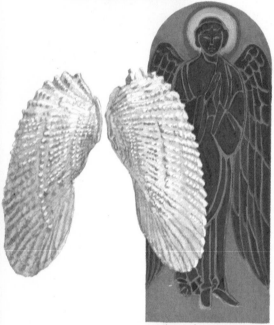

Angel wings

Moon shell

Top shell

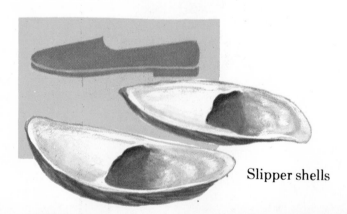

Slipper shells

Shells are really one-room houses. Each shell has room for just one kind of animal. Scientists call the little animals *mollusks*.

Although most mollusks live in the water, some are found on land. This snail lives in the forest and lays its eggs in the ground. In the picture the eggs have been very much enlarged so that you can see them, for they are very tiny.

When they are born, mollusks do not have backbones like other animals. Most of them have very little bony stuff. They are soft and squishy and helpless. Mollusks need protection from enemies that would eat them. They get this protection from the shell they build around themselves. Mollusks can build a house out of their own bodies.

Of course, baby mollusks do not really *build* houses. They *grow* houses. (It is as easy for them to do this as it is for you to grow fingernails.)

Mollusks eat the tiny bits of food that float with the moving seawater. Part of their food is used to build their bodies. The other part is used to build their shells. Mollusks are covered with a kind of thin second skin called a *mantle*. The part of the food that is used to build the shell oozes out on top of the mantle and hardens.

Finally, the mantle is covered by a hard shell. Now the mollusks have protection. A mollusk and its shell will keep on growing as long as the mollusk lives. They have been known to live in their shells and continue adding on to them for as long as 20 years. By then the shell has gotten quite large.

The smaller shell is one year old, about average for this kind of mollusk. The larger shell was lived in and built on to for 20 years.

Most of the time, the shells that we find are empty. The mollusks that lived in them have been eaten by fish or birds, or they have simply died and dried up in the hot sun. But sometimes, especially after a big storm at sea, you will find a mollusk at home. The waves will have lifted the mollusk, shell and all, up onto the beach.

Some of us have a way of calling *all* shells seashells. But all shells are not found in the sea. You can find shells on riverbanks and on lakefronts. You can find shells at the edge of ponds and streams. There are shells to be found in rain forests, and you may even find them in your backyard.

The Legless Wonders

It squirms, it wriggles.
It can glide and shake.
It's a legless wonder—
It's a *snake!*
You might think that this green garden snake is about to get
tangled up in its own tail. But it isn't. Wriggling and slithering,
this snake goes exactly where it wants to go.

Fish use their fins and tails to wriggle through water. And
snakes certainly have tails. Except for its head, you could say that
the rest of a snake *is* a tail. At least, it looks that way. But
snakes don't have fins. They don't have legs.

Then how do they move?

Snakes have scales. They wouldn't be able to move much without them. Their long bodies loop, and the scales push against the ground. Twisting and turning, snakes gracefully glide along, over rocks and logs, and even through mud and sand.

Snakes *look* slippery and slimy. But they're not. Their skin actually feels like cool, soft leather.

Here's another thing about a snake's skin—it comes off!

When *you* grow, your skin grows, too. But not a snake's. As a snake gets bigger, its skin gets tighter and tighter until the snake wiggles right out of it—wearing a new skin that it has grown. The old skin turns inside out as the snake crawls out of it, so that it looks like the old skin has come off backwards. A snake sheds its skin a few times a year.

Most snakes won't hurt you if you leave them alone. Even some of the most dangerous of these long, twisting reptiles are so afraid of people that they will wriggle away as fast as they can if they see you first.

Snakes can't travel very far in cold weather. Their bodies become too stiff to move. So if you see any snakes taking an early morning sunbath on a rock, they're probably trying to get warm. After the snakes are warm enough, they will slither away and crawl under a shady rock or log.

In places where the winter is cold, snakes hide between rocks or under the ground. They sleep their long, special sleep called *hibernation.*

In some kinds of snakes the eggs hatch inside the mother snake's body. In other kinds the eggs hatch outside in a nest the snake makes for them in leaves or rotten wood or warm sand. When the babies are born, they wriggle and crawl away to find their own food.

Some snakes are as small as worms. Some are so large they can swallow a goat or a pig whole!

Most snakes live on the land, but some live in trees and others in the water.

All snakes are good hunters. They must be, in order to live. Instead of eating grass, fruit, roots, or vegetables, small snakes eat grasshoppers, beetles, and other bugs and insects. Large snakes eat mice and rats. Still bigger ones eat squirrels and rabbits. The huge snakes could eat a small deer if they could catch one. Some snakes even eat other snakes.

There are biting snakes and squeezing snakes. Some snakes catch their food by biting it. Others catch it by wrapping themselves around it and squeezing it. Snakes don't chew their food. They just swallow it whole. After they have eaten, some snakes rest for two or three days.

Snakes aren't the only hunters, of course. At the same time *they* are hunting, some other animals are hunting them.

There are snakes that eat birds and the eggs of birds. And there are birds that eat snakes, too. Eagles, hawks, owls, and other large birds are among the worst enemies that snakes have. The big birds dive from the sky silently and swiftly to catch a snake before it knows the bird is there. Wild hogs catch snakes by stamping on them, and then they eat them.

The greatest snake fighter of all is probably a thick-furred little animal called a *mongoose*. It can move so fast that it can jump back from the strike of a giant cobra snake and then jump in and kill the cobra. If you live where cobras live, it is a good thing to have a mongoose for a pet.

Some of the greatest snake fighters are snakes themselves. Farmers and other persons who live in places where there are poisonous snakes like to have king snakes and black snakes near their houses. The king snakes and black snakes kill or chase away poisonous snakes.

If you go where snakes are: WATCH OUT . . . BE CAREFUL! It's true that many snakes won't hurt you. But other snakes are dangerous. Some even have needlelike fangs in their mouths. The fangs could punch holes in your skin if a snake bit you, and put poison into your blood. The poison is so bad that it can kill people.

So if you are in snake country, don't reach under a log or a rock.

If you are walking through bushes or brush, carry a stick to poke ahead of you. The movement and sound will usually frighten away any snake that might be there.

Most people who are bitten by snakes are bitten in the leg below the knee. So if you wear high boots in snake country, they will be a great protection.

Don't go wading or swimming in water where poisonous snakes are known to live.

Among the most dangerous snakes are rattlesnakes. They have rattles on the ends of their tails. They shake the rattles when they are alarmed. Rattles sound a little like pebbles being shaken fast in a wooden box. If you ever hear this sound, move away quickly.

Most snakes don't rattle—not even all rattlesnakes do. So when you are in snake country: WATCH OUT . . . BE CAREFUL.

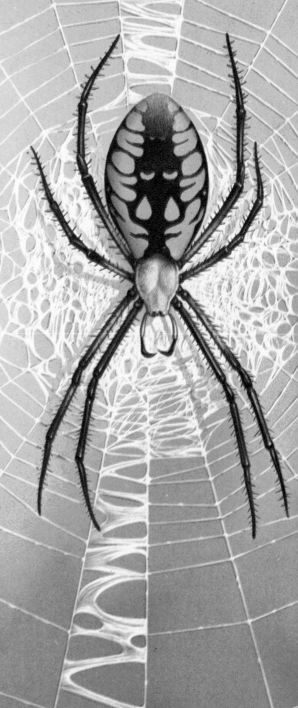

The Spinning Spider

"Won't you come into my parlor?" said the spider to the fly.

Sitting on a soft cushion of silk in its web, this *golden garden spider* will wait . . . and wait . . . and wait. A breeze might sway the lacy nest, but this won't bother the spider.

Food is what this remarkable creature is waiting for so patiently. When a bug gets caught in the web, then the spider will move. Before a bug has time to do more than wiggle and squirm, the spider will rush out and spin some threads of silk around it to hold it tight and then crawl back to its soft, silken pillow to wait again.

Not all spiders make webs to catch food. Some, such as the *jumping spider,* pounce like a cat to capture insects. The big *wolf spider* chases insects on its long, spindly legs. The little *crab spider* hides between flower petals and grabs the insects that come to find nectar.

All spiders spin silk. They have a special spinning "factory" under their stomachs. With their *spinnerets*—which look like short fingers—they spin silk from a watery stuff that comes out through small holes. When it touches the air, the liquid silk changes into silk thread.

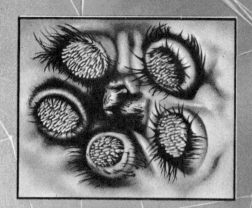

For lining their nests and for their webs, spiders spin strong, smooth silk. For trapping food in their webs, they spin sticky silk. Some spiders spin little bags of soft, fluffy silk to hold the eggs from which new spiders are born.

And suppose a spider is hurrying to escape from an enemy. It quickly spins a getaway thread to climb down on and then scurries away.

Spiders don't fly in airplanes when they want to take a trip. But some will climb to the tip of a leaf or a blade of grass, spin some threads, and wait for the wind to pick them up as if they were bits of dandelion fluff. The spiders float with the silken threads over fields and trees. When they come down, maybe they will be in a place where there are more flies and insects to catch.

Except in icy places or on high mountaintops, spiders live everywhere—even under the ground and under the water.

One underwater spider swims to the bottom of a pond or a stream and builds a silk house shaped like a thimble. It stores food there and the eggs that will hatch into new *water spiders*.

But the water spider can't breathe under water the way a fish can. It has to breathe the same kind of air that other spiders do—the same kind that *you* do.

Do you think it finds this air under the water?

It doesn't. It swims to the top of the water and brings air down in bubbles. It puts the bubbles of air in its underwater house. Then, whenever the spider wants to stay under the water a long time, it goes into its house and breathes the air it carried down in bubbles.

Furry, brown wolf spiders don't build a web or even a nest. They hide under leaves and grass. The mother spider drags her silken bag full of spider eggs with her wherever she goes. When the eggs hatch, the newborn babies climb onto her back and stay there until they can take care of themselves.

Spiders have eight legs. If they lose a leg, most spiders can grow a new one! Some spiders have as many as eight eyes. Some have one kind of eyes for seeing in the daytime and a different kind for seeing at night.

The biggest spider is bigger than your hand. Much bigger. Big enough to eat a bird! That's what it's called—a *bird spider*. Surprising as it might seem, this giant of the spiders isn't very dangerous to people. When bothered, it pinches a little with its mouth, but that's about all. Some people even keep it for a pet.

Spiders help us by destroying many harmful insects. And some spiders build beautiful webs. Most spiders won't hurt us. But a few will.

The *black widow spider* is little and shiny and black. It has a tiny, bright red mark on it. It lives under stones or under the bark of a tree or wherever it's dark and damp. It has a dangerous, poisonous bite.

BEWARE! WATCH OUT! THESE SPIDERS ARE DANGEROUS!

The *brown recluse spider* is small, too. It has a dark, violin-shaped spot on its head. But the spot is hard to see, and the brown spider looks very much like some other spiders. It spins its web in warm, dry places, such as attics or barns, and it is almost as dangerous as the black widow spider.

The *tarantula* can hurt you if it bites you. It looks frightening because it is very big. It's scary and hairy. But its bite is not nearly so dangerous as that of the black widow spider or the brown spider.

The Sun and Its Planets

This is a picture of the Earth. Not as we usually see it, because we see only a little bit of the Earth when we're looking from our houses or even from the top of a very tall building.

But this is how the Earth might look from far out in space—the way it looks to astronauts as they travel to the moon.

Here is another picture of the Earth. But this time it looks much smaller. If we traveled many millions of miles out into space—even farther than astronauts do—the Earth would appear this tiny.

This is how the Earth would look if we were many, many *millions* of miles out in space (it's the small ball with the arrow pointing to it). The sun looks about the size of a dime. And the round object with rings around it is Saturn. Saturn and Earth are *planets*. They move around the sun. There are seven other planets, too—nine all together. The sun and the planets are part of what is called the *solar system*.

Now, just suppose we could travel—not millions and millions of miles—but millions and millions and *millions* and *billions* of miles away from the Earth and the rest of our solar system.

Can you find the red arrow in this picture? It's pointing at a tiny star in the sky. That tiny star is what our sun would look like if we could travel all those millions and billions of miles. The Earth and all the other planets would be so small that you couldn't even see them!

Imagine being so far from home and seeing that small star that is our sun and saying,

> Star light,
> Star bright,
> First star I see tonight. . . .

More About the Sun

All the big planets in our solar system travel around the sun at different speeds. As they move in their paths, or *orbits*, around the sun, the planets also spin around like tops.

As the Earth spins, the part of it that faces the sun has daylight. The part that faces away from the sun has night. (When it's day in New York City, it's night in Tokyo, Japan.)

As far as we know, there are no living things on any planet except Earth, though no one can say for certain. The Earth's distance from the sun gives our planet exactly the amount of heat and light that plants and animals need for life. If you look carefully at the picture, you'll be able to see which planet is closest to the sun. It's *Mercury*

Venus is the brightest planet and is sometimes called the *evening star*.

328

On certain nights you can see the planet *Mars*, which looks something like a red star in the sky.

Jupiter is the largest planet.

Saturn has three rings around it, which are made of many bits, or *particles*.

Uranus is visible only when the skies are very clear.

Neptune is so far from the sun—and so dark—that we can't see it without a telescope.

Pluto is farthest away from the sun.

When we have learned more about our solar system and space travel, we may be able to visit other planets.

Anyone for a trip to Mars?

Different Ways to Tell Time

How could we tell time if there were no watches or clocks anywhere in the world?

The sun was probably the world's first "clock," except in the far north, where the Eskimos live. There, it's dark most of the winter, and light most of the summer. But in most of the world, people have used the sun for a clock. Even today, if you don't have a regular clock that shows time, you still know that when the sun shines, it's day, and when it's dark, it's night.

Not only can the sun tell you whether it's day or night but also whether it's morning, noon, or afternoon. When the sun is almost directly overhead, it's noon. When the sun is halfway to this point, it's the middle of the morning. When it's halfway down again, it's the middle of the afternoon.

Have you ever noticed that your shadow is longest in the early morning and in the late afternoon? At noon, when the sun is overhead, there is little or no shadow. A long time ago, people noticed the way that shadows kept changing as the sun's place in the sky changed. Do you know what they did about it? They made a sun clock, or a *sundial,* as we call it today.

When the sun shines on a sundial, a piece of metal sticking up on the sundial makes a shadow. As the sun's place in the sky changes, the shadow on the sundial changes. The shadow touches different numbers in somewhat the same way as the hands of a clock point to numbers. It is almost as easy to read the time on a sundial as it is on a clock.

But what if the sun isn't shining and there are no shadows anywhere?

People who live near the ocean can tell time from the tides. In the daytime, for about six hours, the water rises higher and higher on the beach. And then it goes down and down for about six hours. The same thing happens again at night. There are two high tides and two low tides every 24 hours.

Sailors on a ship learn how to tell time by looking at the moon and the stars. The whole sky is their clock!

In some places in the world the wind comes up at about the same time every day or changes direction or stops blowing. In these places the wind can be the clock!

A can of water can help you measure time!

Get someone to punch a tiny hole in the bottom of a can. Then fill the can with water.

The water will come *drip-drip* out of the can. You will have a water clock.

Each time you fill the can right to the top, it will take about the same amount of time for the water to drip out. If you told a friend that you could play for only two more emptyings of your water clock, you both would know exactly when to stop playing.

A sand clock is an even better clock.

If you had fine dry sand in a glass shaped like the one in the picture, you would have what is called an *hourglass*. The sand in an hourglass flows from the top part to the bottom part in exactly one hour. When the hourglass is turned over, the sand will take another hour to flow back again.

Other kinds of sand clocks, called *egg timers,* look like tiny hourglasses. The sand inside egg timers falls to the bottom in the time that it takes to boil an egg.

How Do Babies Travel?

Some babies travel in fancy four-wheeled carriages, snuggled down in soft comforters.

Some travel in strollers, watching people and birds and dogs as they ride.

But not all babies travel in carriages or strollers. Parents may carry their babies in other ways.

334

Babies of some Arctic Eskimo families stay safe and warm in a special pouch sewn into the back of the mother's jacket. An Eskimo jacket is called a *parka*.

In some Eskimo families, the mother makes all of the clothes for her family from the skins of reindeer, seals, bears, and other animals. The animals are trapped by the men of the family. Eskimos still hunt, but today they usually sell the animals' fur and buy clothes and other supplies in stores.

When the American Indians roamed the lands, the baby, called the *papoose*, was carried strapped to the mother's back. The baby's carrying place was sometimes woven from grasses and twigs. Sometimes it was a basket. Sometimes the Indian baby was strapped to a flat board, which was then tied to the mother's back. The softened furry skins of animals could be laced together to keep the baby snug and dry.

When the mother stopped to rest, the cradle-basket could be hung in a tree so that the wind could rock the baby.

The father pipefish is the one who takes care of the babies in the pipefish family. He is so long and thin that he looks almost like a snake. He has a *pouch,* or pocket, where he carries his babies. Baby pipefishes get a slow ride in their pocket home, for their father is not a fast swimmer.

Another baby that lives in a pocket is the kangaroo. What a hoppy ride these babies get! Their mothers leap fast and far.

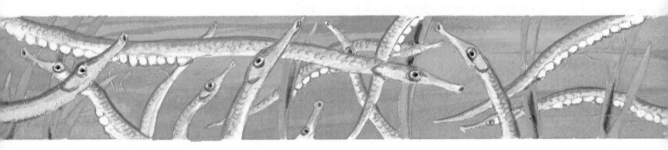

Most baby opossums get to ride in a stomach pouch when they are small. But some baby opossums are carried on their mother's back. Opossums like to hang from things. They can sleep hanging from a tree by their tails. It is easy for them to cling to their mother as she ambles along. The mother bends her tail back. The babies wind their tails around hers and dig their feet into her soft fur.

A bat baby flies through the air as it rides on its mother's back. The mother bat flies at night, searching for insects which she catches in the air. She often takes her babies with her. They cling to her furry neck with their tiny sharp claws. Wouldn't *that* be fun for the baby—to go sailing through the air on its mother's back!

Some monkey babies have almost as much fun. Their mothers carry them wherever they go. High above the ground, the mothers travel from tree to tree, leaping and swinging from one branch to another. Sometimes you can see them doing this at a zoo.

Even a mouth can be a handy place to carry a baby! The sea catfish father carries his newborn youngsters around in his mouth.

And did you ever watch a mother cat or dog move her children? Or a lioness at a zoo? She uses her mouth—picking up her babies by the loose skin on the back of the neck.

The men who drive camels across the deserts have a special way for camel babies to be carried. When it travels in a caravan, a baby camel rides in a cloth sling on the side of another camel. The mother camel is next in line, so she can always see her baby. When the caravan stops, the mother camel nurses her baby.

Where Is Everybody?

Everybody here is trying to get somewhere faster by going into a tunnel. There are many kinds of tunnels. This tunnel is an underground shortcut that we can use to go from one place to another.

In the world of tunnels, the trains and automobiles go speeding
under hills and mountains and even under rivers.

Trains rush through city tunnels called *subways*. The trains roar
like thunder as they go through the tunnel. When the train stops
at the station where you are waiting, you have to step inside
quickly, or the doors will close and the train will leave
without you.

How did the tunnels get where they are?

If you have ever tried to make a tunnel in snow, you know how
quickly the snow can cave in . . . and no more tunnel!

When men make tunnels under the ground, they use machines
to cut through hard rock, and they build strong walls to hold the
dirt and water back. They wear special helmets so that they won't
be hurt if rocks fall on their heads.

Some tunnels are built through high mountains. The tunnel is the shortest way through. Men used to build roads *over* the mountains instead. Or, if a mountain was *too* tall or the sides went up too straight, the road was built around the sides.

These roads were sometimes dangerous and long and hard to drive.

The tunnel is safer, easier, and shorter.

Some tunnels are built for cars or trains to use. Others are built for people to walk through.

Often tunnels are built under city streets so that trains, cars, or people can go from one place to another without getting caught in the slow-moving traffic of the city streets.

Some tunnels are built under rivers. They let trains or cars go from one side of the river to the other. If the tunnel is deep enough under the water, ships can easily sail over the tunnel.

Men have learned how to make and use tunnels, but some animals were making and using them long before people were. Both gophers and moles build underground tunnels and live in them.

The tools that the small, soft-furred mole uses for digging are its large front feet, shaped like shovels. The mole spends most of its life underground, in the tunnels it digs.

The Turtle Takes Its Time

These baby sea turtles climbing out of their eggs won't need a mother or father turtle to help them. They will be able to take care of themselves. They will scramble from their nest under the sand and walk on their tiny new flippers to the water.

When they're grown, these sea turtles will come back to shore to make their own nests. Because they can't live in hot sunshine for very long, they will dig their nests after sunset and then lay their eggs and cover them with sand. Later, after they have rested, they will return to the sea.

When the babies are hatched, they, too, will take care of themselves, finding their way to the sea and to the small fish, snails, and insects that they eat.

This is the way all turtles start life—alone and on land.

Although turtles start life alone, they are always at home because they carry their houses with them wherever they go. Their houses are their shells! Always tough as leather, sometimes hard as rocks, the shells help keep the turtles safe from enemies.

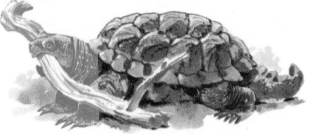

If you picked up a little box turtle, it would pull its head, legs, and tail all the way inside its shell. Box turtles aren't dangerous, and they make good pets.

Don't get too close to a snapping turtle. Its jaws are strong. When it bites anything, it hangs on for a long time and won't let go.

Many turtles live in oceans, ponds, or muddy river bottoms. But some don't live in water at all. Some live in hot desert sands, miles and miles away from water. They dig under the ground to protect themselves from the hot sun.

Other turtles live in damp woods, stretching their long necks out from their shells to look for insects under logs and to reach the leaves, green shoots, and berries that they eat.

But no matter where they live, turtles don't need to hunt for food or water all the time. They have a special place inside their bodies where they can store water. And they can store food in the form of fat. Turtles can live for days, even weeks, without anything to eat or drink.

There are turtles as small as a child's hand. Others, like the leatherback turtle, weigh as much as a small elephant. For their size, turtles are among the slowest-moving animals. All of them live longer than any other animal we know about.

Since the days when there were dinosaurs, turtles have roamed the Earth, both on land and in water. But in all these millions of years, they haven't changed very much.

The Soda Pop Volcano

Let's talk about soda pop.
Soda pop is water,
   flavoring,
      sweetening,
         and gas—all mixed up together.
In a bottle the glass presses against the soda pop from all sides and keeps it quiet.

When you take the cap off, some of the gas escapes with a *z-z-zip* and pushes some of the soda pop out with it in spatters and bubbles.

Now let's talk about volcanoes.

In a volcano, melted rock and gas are all mixed up together. (Most of it is not the same kind of gas that's in soda pop, but still it's gas.)

Deep in the earth the hard rock presses against the melted rock and gas from all sides and keeps it quiet.

But if the melted rock and gas comes near the top of the ground, some of the gas sometimes escapes with a *z-z-zip* through a hole and pushes some of the melted rock out with it.

So you could say that a volcano is a little like a bottle of soda pop . . . or that a bottle of soda pop is a little like a volcano.

The Smoking Mountain

A few years ago men on a ship in the ocean saw the water bubbling and boiling. They went closer. Night came before they had seen very much. But in the morning they saw an island where there had been no island before.

It was a very hot island, with smoke, steam, and fire.

Actually, the island was the top of a mountain that had been growing up from the floor of the ocean and had poked through the water into the air.

How does a mountain grow?

If the mountain is a volcano, it is easy to see how it grows. A volcano starts from a hole in the ground from which hot rock and smoke and steam come out. Far, far under the ground it is so hot that rock melts. This hot melted rock, or *lava,* is sometimes pushed out of the earth through a hole or a crack in the ground. The steam inside the earth pushes the rock out.

As more and more rock comes out, it makes a pile that becomes a mountain. Sometimes the rock flows out like hot mush. Sometimes it is shot out in big chunks of hard rock. The more stuff that comes out, the higher the mountain grows.

If the mountain is growing under the ocean, it becomes an island when it reaches the top of the water. The little island that the men saw from the ship started this way. So did the big Hawaiian Islands and the enormous island of Iceland.

Not many years ago in Mexico, a little boy and his father discovered a volcano growing in a cornfield. Smoke puffed up, and rock started popping up out of a crack that opened in the ground.

The boy thought the cornfield was throwing rocks at him! He picked one up. It was hot. He dropped it and ran away frightened. Smoke and rock continued to come from the crack in the ground.

A new volcano was being born.

The volcano in the cornfield grew until it was bigger than the cornfield! Black smoke puffed out. Hot ashes fell like black snowflakes. Hot rock and fire and lava shot out. People called the volcano the Little Monster because it grew so fast. Scientists came from all over the world to study it and watch it grow. It is not often that people get a chance to watch a volcano from the very beginning.

Most of the volcanoes have been here for a very long time. Some have been here so long that now they are cold. They are called dead volcanoes. They have stopped throwing out fire and melted rock and smoke. It is safe to walk on them. Farms are plowed on the quiet slopes, and people have built houses there.

Some volcanoes have stopped throwing out hot rock, but they still smoke a little now and then. They are "sleeping" volcanoes. Sometime they may "wake up."

A volcano named Vesuvius slept for a thousand years. But it woke up and threw out so much hot melted rock that it buried the buildings of two cities.

Today volcanoes are not so dangerous for people as they were a long time ago. Now we know more about *why* volcanoes do what they do, and we can usually tell *when* they are going to do it. Before a sleeping volcano wakes up, it usually makes a noise like faraway thunder, and the ground shakes in small earthquakes. People are warned and have time to get away safely.

People used to think dragons under the earth caused volcanoes. They said the smoke that puffed above the ground was the dragon's breath. They said the earthquakes were caused by the dragon's moving around down in the earth. Now we know that this is not true.

Another thing we know about volcanoes is that they don't happen just anywhere. There are certain places under the earth

354

where the rock is broken in a way that lets the steam and hot rock escape to the outside more easily. Scientists know where these places are, and maps have been made to let everybody know.

There are different kinds of volcanoes. Some explode so violently that the rock goes high into the air and falls miles away. A volcano may shoot out ashes so high that they float all the way around the world. They have made the sunsets green and the snow purple.

Other volcanoes are more gentle. The hot lava rises in their cones and overflows, rolling slowly down the mountainside, where it becomes cool and hard.

One very tall volcano stays fiery red at the top all the time. It is lucky that the volcano is near the ocean. Sailors can use it for a lighthouse.

Big Winds

Big winds can be fun. They blow the branches of trees around and rattle the windows. If they're not too strong, they are great for flying kites and making sailboats go.

But there are some big winds that are too big for safety—hurricanes and tornadoes.

A hurricane begins over the ocean in the hot parts of the world when strong winds coming from opposite directions bump into each other. These winds start whirling around.

The sky becomes dark with whirling clouds that look like a giant wheel.

The center of a hurricane is a very calm place. Weathermen call this place the *eye* of the hurricane. In the eye the wind is light and the big puffy clouds do not whirl around.

Sometimes a ship will battle its way through the strong winds and high seas that go with a hurricane. When it comes to the eye, some of the people on the ship may think the hurricane is over . . . when *whoops!* Here comes the other half!

If the hurricane hits land, it can be very bad. The winds of a hurricane are strong enough to blow down trees and houses. The hurricane also stirs up the ocean into big waves. When the waves hit the land, they can wreck docks and roads along the shore.

Sometimes hurricanes cause heavy rainstorms. The rain may flood creeks and rivers, making them overflow into places where they shouldn't be. A river is a nice place to fish, but when it moves into your living room—look out! Or you'll get wet feet. And wet furniture. You might even have to crawl out on the roof!

Because hurricanes are dangerous and can cause much trouble, the weathermen have worked out a system of hurricane watchers.

Some of these watchers are on ships at sea. When hurricane watchers find out that a hurricane is starting, they radio the weathermen back on the land.

Men are then sent out in airplanes to look for the hurricane. When these flyers find the storm, they fly right into it to find the eye. By using scientific equipment on the plane, they learn how fast the winds are going around and how fast the storm is moving toward the land.

The weathermen know days ahead of time that a hurricane is coming. Then they tell the radio and television announcers and the newspapermen, who, in turn, tell the people.

When they know that a hurricane is coming, people have time to board up their windows so that the winds won't break the glass. They can stay away from the beaches where the big storm waves

will come crashing. They can make dams of sandbags to keep river water out of their living rooms.

After a hurricane has hit land, the circle of winds begins to fall apart. That's why you will never see a hurricane if you live a long way from the ocean. By the time a hurricane gets far inland, it isn't a hurricane any longer—it's just an ordinary thunderstorm or a big wind.

Another kind of big wind is called a *tornado*. A tornado comes whirling over the land instead of the ocean. Tornadoes are much, much smaller storms than hurricanes. And, while a hurricane may last for days and days as it moves across the open ocean, a tornado may last only an hour or so.

Like a hurricane, a tornado is made up of winds going around and around in a circle. But the circle of a tornado is very small compared with the wind wheel of a hurricane.

As you can see by the picture, a tornado looks very much like a funnel. Of course, you can't see the wind. What you see is the dirt that the tornado snatches up from the ground and whirls in the air.

The whirling winds of a tornado spin around much faster than those of a hurricane. The winds whirl like a top or like the water in a bucket when you take a stick and stir the water very fast. If an airplane tried to fly into the whirling wind funnel of a tornado, it would be torn into a million bits.

While it is whirling so fast, the funnel of a tornado moves along about as fast as a fast automobile. It twists and turns, now high, now low. It passes by within a few seconds. But within those few seconds it can lift a train off a track, lift an automobile off a road, or pull a big tree out of the ground by the roots.

Weathermen have worked out ways to warn people when a tornado is coming. They keep a close watch on winds and temperatures, especially in the spring and early summer—when tornadoes are most likely to happen. They do not happen everywhere. Most of them blow across the middle part of the United States, where the land is flat.

If the weathermen decide that the weather conditions might produce tornadoes, they tell the radio and television announcers, who then tell the people. The announcers also tell the people the best ways to protect themselves from a tornado:

If you are in a house with a basement, go to the basement and stay in the corner that is nearest the coming tornado.

If you have a real storm cellar, go into that.

If you are out in the open, run for a low place or a ditch and lie flat.

If you are in a house where there is no basement, stay away from the windows and doors. Leave a few windows open. This lets the winds blow through the house instead of breaking the windows or something else.

As soon as the danger of a tornado is over, the announcers will hear the good news from the weathermen and tell the people.

What's a Cloud?

Did you ever look up at a soft white cloud and think, "Wouldn't it be fun if I could bounce around on it and lie back in its white softness and take a ride through the sky?"

Have you ever wondered what they are—those big, white, lumpy things moving around in the sky?

Well, what *are* they? You know they're not marshmallows or cotton or soapsuds. But did you know they are *water*? Hundreds and thousands of gallons of water, floating high in the air.

Does that seem hard to believe—that water floats in the air?

Well, it does, even though the water is in such tiny droplets that you couldn't see one even if it were separated from all the others.

It takes billions of tiny droplets to make a big cloud.

Now that you know that clouds are really great clumps of water droplets you can begin to see how clouds bring rain.

Sometimes the water droplets form around tiny pieces of dust in the air.

These droplets with dust in them get bigger and bigger as they join together until they become too heavy to float and they fall—plop!

And that's rain!

But you know that clouds don't *always* bring rain. And clouds don't always look like soapsuds or marshmallows. There are two main kinds of rainy clouds—tall, tall, cottony ones like these on this page.

And flat, gray, dismal-looking ones like these.

The tall, white, cottony rainclouds are called *thunderheads* because they lift their heads so high and they often bring thunderstorms. They also have a big scientific name—*cumulo-nimbus*. The flat gray ones are called *nimbostratus*.

Besides rain, there are other things that fall from clouds: snow and sleet and hail. Snow and sleet fall only on a cold winter day, but hailstones can fall even on a warm summer day.

Sometimes a cloud is *so* high, where the air is *so* cold, that the whole cloud is made of ice—tiny bright specks of ice floating in the air—instead of tiny drops of water. You can tell these clouds when you see them. They are called *cirrus* clouds and they look like these wispy clouds in the bright blue sky.

If you ride in an airplane, you may get very close to a cloud. You may even go right through one. It's like going through fog. In fact, that's about what a cloud is—fog floating high in the air. Or would you say a fog is just a cloud sitting on the ground?

A cloud can't move by itself. Winds carry clouds through the sky. Sometimes when you don't even feel a breeze, you see the clouds moving. Then you know that winds are blowing high up in the air.

But where do clouds come from, anyway?

When the sun dries up a puddle of water, where does the puddle go? Up!—up into the air. That's where many of the tiny drops of water in a cloud come from—puddles and ponds and rivers and oceans.

So the next time you see a puddle of water on the street, you can say to yourself, "That's going to be part of a cloud." And the next time you see a cloud, you can say, "There's my puddle starting!"

The Biggest Animal of All

There's something very fishy about whales. They live in the water. They look like fish. They swim like fish.

But they aren't fish at all.

Whales are warm-blooded animals like people and cows and horses. Millions of years ago, their ancestors lived on land. They walked around on four legs and were hairy like other animals.

Then—nobody knows exactly why—they started living more and more in the sea. And finally, they began to look more and more like fish. They lost their hair. And when their bodies became smooth, they could glide through the water easily. Their hind legs also disappeared. They grew a thick layer of fat—called *blubber*—under their skin to keep themselves warm in the cold seas.

With these and a few other changes, they got along very nicely in their watery home.

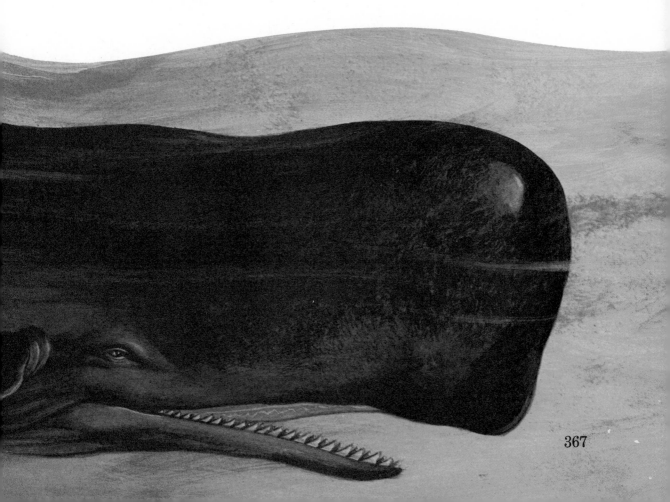

But because whales are not fish, they can't stay under the water all the time as fish do. They have to come up for air once in a while, or they will drown.

When they come up, the first thing they do is blow out the breath they have been holding. When their warm breath hits the colder air, it makes a cloud of mist, just as our breath does when we blow it while outdoors on a cold day. This mist is called the whale's *spout*.

You can spot a whale by its spout.

Sometimes many whales come to the surface and blow at the same time. That is a very fine sight to see.

Another interesting thing happened to whales when they started living in the water. They began to grow bigger and bigger. Some whales are so big now that they couldn't possibly live on land. They would be too heavy to move around. They need the water to hold up part of their great weight.

The biggest whale of all is the blue whale. As far as we know, it is the biggest animal that ever lived. It is much bigger than an elephant. It is bigger than any dinosaur. Even a baby blue whale is a whale of a baby. And the mother whale has to feed it for about six months . . . until it learns to feed itself.

Finding food is a simple matter for blue whales. They just swim along with their huge mouths open, and thousands of tiny sea creatures—some so small that they hardly can be seen—flow in.

Like most of the largest whales, blue whales have no teeth. Instead, they have strings of hardened skin (something like our fingernails) in their mouths. This material is called *baleen*, or *whalebone*. It hangs down in the whale's mouth like a giant comb. The whale can hold thousands of bits of food behind this baleen and strain the salt ocean water out of its mouth.

Most of the smaller whales have teeth. These whales eat fish or any other sea creature they can catch.

One of these smaller whales is the killer whale. (It isn't small compared with other animals. It's small only compared with the giant blue whales.)

The killer whale always has been thought of as a cruel and dangerous animal—the terror of the sea. It eats seals, sea lions, penguins, and even other whales. All fish fear it. Killer whales travel in packs like wolves. They are very fast and strong, and even many sharks are afraid of them. But in recent years a few of the captured killer whales have become good-natured and friendly pets.

Some whales aren't fierce at all. This is especially true of the dolphin, one of the smaller whales. As far back as the ancient days of Greece and Rome, stories were told about dolphins that gave children rides on their backs.

Not many years ago, there was a famous dolphin named Opo who visited the same New Zealand beach almost every day. It played ball with the children in the water and even gave some of them short rides on its back. If one of the big whales would do this, just about everybody in a schoolroom could go for a ride at the same time.

A dolphin named Pelorus Jack used to wait at the harbor entrance to Sydney, Australia, and guide ships safely past the dangerous places in the water.

Now that scientists have begun to study the whole family of whales more carefully, they are amazed at how friendly, playful, and smart many of the whales are. They are learning that whales, like dogs and chimpanzees, can be trained to do many things.

A Very Special Picture

Timmy was a little nervous when he went to the hospital after he fell. His arm hurt, and Dr. Zimm was going to X-ray it.

In the X-ray room, a nurse smiled and asked Timmy to sit in a chair and rest his hurt arm on a table. Then she went over to a big machine.

"Is that going to hurt?" Timmy asked.

When the nurse said it wouldn't, Timmy felt better.

"It's only going to take a picture of the bones in your arm," she said.

"Right through my skin?"

"Yes," she nodded. "X rays," she told Timmy, "can take a picture—a shadow picture—through cloth, leather, wood—even through metal."

"Are they magic?" Timmy asked.

Dr. Zimm had come in, and he said, "No, they're not magic, Timmy. But they *are* very powerful and *can* be dangerous if not used carefully."

The doctor explained that the nurse's apron and gloves were made of rubber mixed with lead, and that this protected her when she worked around the X-ray machine.

"Lead is one thing X rays *can't* go through," the doctor said.

"Will the X rays make my arm better?" Timmy asked.

"No, but the picture will show whether a bone is broken," the doctor said. "If it is, I'll know how to fix it."

The doctor also explained that if someone swallows a pin or a penny, an X-ray picture will show where it is stuck. He said that doctors who take care of pets also use X rays to find out what is wrong with a sick animal. Even tree doctors use X rays when trees aren't healthy. And dentists take X-ray pictures of teeth to find out whether there are any hidden cavities.

"Do only doctors and nurses use X rays?" Timmy asked.

The doctor said no, that in factories some workers use X rays to check the parts of automobiles, airplanes, radios, and many other things.

Then he told Timmy, "We could go into an old building with X rays and find out whether there are pipes and wires behind the walls."

Timmy grew excited. "Or maybe hidden treasure!"

The doctor laughed. "Sure, if there's any there."

"When did X rays ever get started?" Timmy wanted to know. The doctor told him that long ago a man named Wilhelm Roentgen was experimenting with electricity—that means he was trying to do new things with it. While he was running the electricity through a glass tube in which there was a tiny bit of a special gas, he saw a strange glow of light on a screen nearby. When he put his hand between the tube and the screen, he could see the bones of his hand in a shadow picture on the screen. He didn't know what the strange light was. He called it *X rays*. Later, his discovery made him famous and won prizes for him.

When Dr. Zimm looked at the X-ray picture of Timmy's hand, he said, "No broken bones, Timmy. Only a bad bruise. You'll be fine in no time at all."

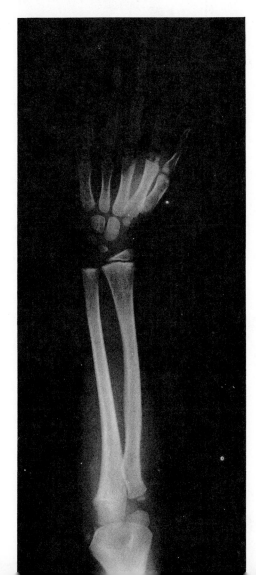

How We Move

Inside our skin there are bones. Our fingers can feel them almost everywhere. One bone is attached to another, and when the bones move, we move.

But our bones cannot move themselves.

Our *muscles* move them.

Our bones are covered with muscles. The muscles move them in many directions. That is the job of muscles—to move things.

How do our muscles move our bones?

Our muscles move our bones by pulling them. Muscles always pull—they never push.

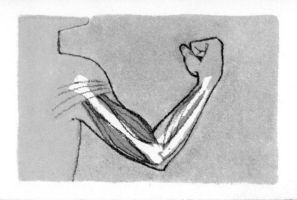

The pink muscle is doing the pulling to bend the arm.

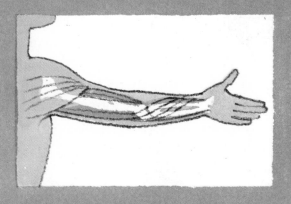

Now a different muscle is pulling to straighten the arm.

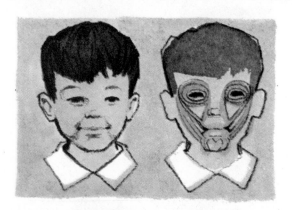

We can feel the jaw muscles in our cheeks become hard as they pull our jaw closed when we bite.

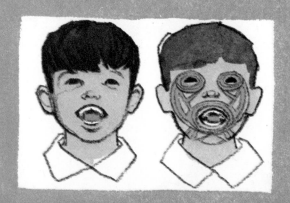

We can feel the muscle under our jaw pull to open our mouth wide.

Some muscles don't move
bones. They move *other* things.

Our heart is the muscle that
pumps the blood. To understand
how it works, imagine a few
children standing in a circle with
their arms hooked together. If
they all *pull* at the same time,
what happens?

They squeeze the circle smaller.

When the heart squeezes like
this, the blood is pumped out
and through the body.

376

Tiny muscles move our eyes up, down, and from side to side.

The muscles of our mouth, lips, and face move to make us smile or frown.

Without muscles the skin would be like a bag. And a man would be a bag of bones!

Using Your Head

I think about the reason why
The sun and moon are in the sky
And how the tears drip from my eye
And how a kite can fly so high.

I think about the reason for
The seeds inside an apple core
And how the waves get to the shore
And how a lion roars its roar.

Did you ever stop to think about *why* you can think? Or *how* you think? Or how important it is to think?

Long ago, cavemen learned to make sparks by hitting two special rocks together. These sparks made fire. When the fire spread to the forest and burned the things the cavemen needed for food, they learned that they had to be careful with fire. They also learned that fire does not burn water, so they used the water to put out small fires. And they learned to hide in the water during large fires.

After the cavemen taught their children how to make fire, the children knew something that had taken their parents years to learn. The children then had time to learn new things and time to find out better ways to do old things. Soon they knew more than their parents did—because they knew the things their parents had taught them, and they knew the things they had figured out for themselves.

When someone says, "Use your head," he really means, "Use your brain." Your brain is inside your head.

Your brain does many different things. One thing it does is to find out what's happening outside your body and what the things outside your body are like.

To do this the brain depends on your eyes, ears, nose, tongue, and skin. These helpers send messages to the brain through many thin, stringlike things called *nerves*.

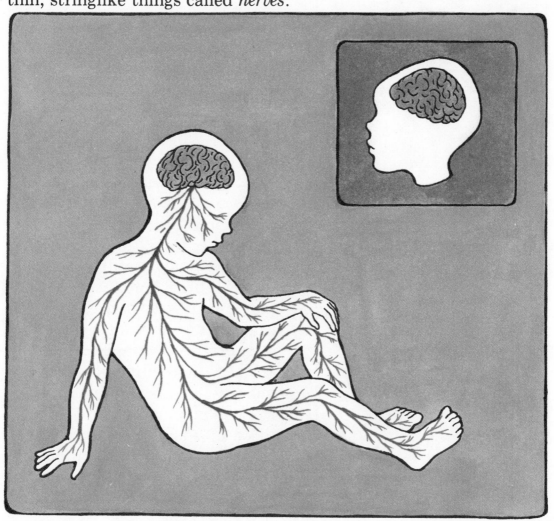

If your mother gives you a bowl of fresh strawberries, your eyes see the plump red berries and your nose smells the good strawberry smell. These messages go to your brain through the nerves, and you know that there are strawberries for you to eat.

When you spoon some of the berries into your mouth, your tongue sends a message to the brain about the delicious taste. The skin in your mouth sends a message about how good the juicy strawberries feel between your teeth and your tongue. Your ears send a message about the sound of your spoon scraping in the bowl.

Another thing the brain does is to make the parts of the body move. When your mother sets the bowl of strawberries in front of you, your brain gets the message from your eyes and nose.

Then the brain makes the muscles in your arm and hand work to pick up your spoon, scoop up some strawberries, put them into your mouth, and take the spoon out again.

Then your brain makes the muscles in your jaw move to chew and makes those in your throat move to swallow.

To move your muscles the brain sends messages through other nerves. These nerves go to every muscle in your body.

Think of all the things you see, hear, smell, taste, feel, and do each day. What a busy brain you have!

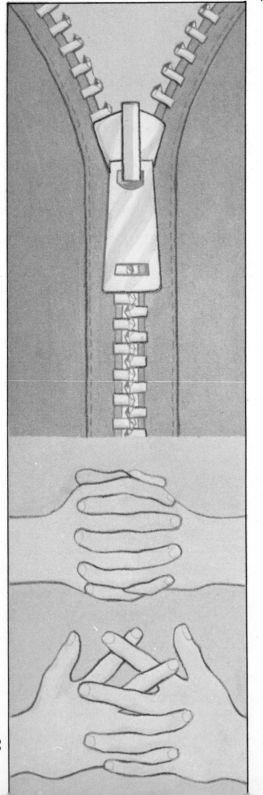

How Do They Work?

Can you hook your fingers together? See—that's the way a zipper works. It's hard to pull your hands apart when your fingers are hooked together. Your zipper holds together in the same way.

Now unhook one pair of fingers. Your hands start to come apart. That's how a zipper opens.

Let's look closely at a zipper. All along each side of the zipper are little "fingers" clamped to a tape. On the top of each finger is a little bump that fits into a hollow at the bottom of the opposite finger.

Zip! Zip! You zip the zippers. Your boots are closed—or your snowsuit. It's almost like magic.

What "magic" thing fits the zipper bumps into the hollows? A slide that goes up the middle of the zipper, guiding the bump of one finger into the hollow of the other. That's how the zipper closes.

When the slide goes down the middle, separating every bump from its hollow, the zipper opens.

When your grandparents were children, zippers were not yet widely used. Then how did jackets and boots and dresses fasten together? With buckles, buttons, hooks, and snaps. About 70 years ago, people with new ideas thought up better ways to fasten things. The zipper, or slide fastener, was invented. And ever since, people have been finding ways to make better zippers— and more uses for zippers.

Zippers for sleeping bags,
   Zippers for suits,
Zippers for purses,
   And zippers for boots.

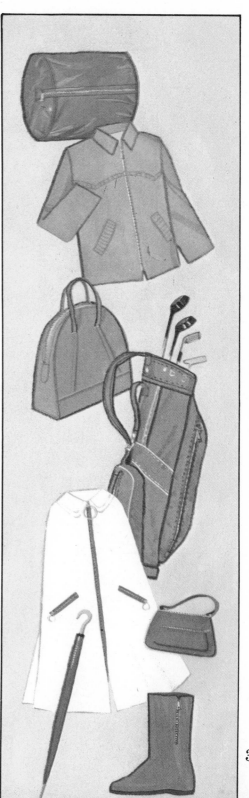

CREDITS

Staff Writers

John Dennis
Ryerson Johnson
Bonnie Nims
Joan Zucker

Contributing Writers

Otto Binder
Margaret Bjorck
Jack Bryson
Barbara Byhouwer
Mary Jane Engh
Frances Gies
Gene Klinger
Margaret Knowles
Jeanette Lerner
Katherine D. Marko
Roberta Postma
Alice Means Reeve
Lloyd Eric Reeve
Jerianne Roginski
Carol Stevenson
Jeanne Murray Walker

Artists

Roy Anderson
George Armstrong
Peggy Chapman
David Cook
Gino D'Achille
Carolyn Dinan
Alex Ebel
J. Finnell
Larry Fredericks
Betty Fraser
Michael Hampshire
Alice Hauser
Michael Heslop
Roberta House
Edwin Huff
Herb Kane
Dick Keane
Earnie Kollar
Dora Leder
Don Madden
Donald Meighan
Erica Merkling
Gary Meyer
Chuck Mitchell
Susan Perl
Rod Ruth
Al Stine
George Suyeoka
Richard Thompson
Jane Walworth
Jan Wills
Muriel Wood